A WOMAN

A PLAN

AN OUTLINE

OF A MAN

ESSAYS

by

SARAH KASBEER

ZONE 3 PRESS
Clarksville, Tennessee

Copyright ©2020 by Sarah Kasbeer

Library of Congress Cataloging-in-Publication Data

Names: Kasbeer, Sarah, 1982- author.

Title: A woman, a man, an outline of a plan : essays / by Sarah Kasbeer.

Description: Clarksville, Tennessee : Zone 3 Press, [2020] |

Identifiers: LCCN 2020024747 (print) | LCCN 2020024748 (ebook) | ISBN
9781733150514 (trade paperback) | ISBN 9781733150521 (ebook)

LC record available at https://lccn.loc.gov/2020024747
LC ebook record available at https://lccn.loc.gov/2020024748

ISBN: 9781733150514

Book Design by David Bieloh
Cover Design by Patrick Gosnell

AP Austin Peay State University

Austin Peay State University does not discriminate on the basis of race, color, religion,
creed, national origin, sex, sexual orientation, gender identity/expression, disability, age,
status as a protected veteran, genetic information, or any other legally protected class
with respect to all employment, programs and activities sponsored by APSU. https://
www.apsu.edu/policy. Policy 6:003. AP11/7-20/200/SpencerPrinting/Honesdale,PA

You are so many years late,
Nevertheless I am glad you came.

—*Anna Ahkmatova*

CONTENTS

ON THE EDGE OF SEVENTEEN

Tammy drove a black pickup, smaller than her son Jack's blue one, which sat idly in their driveway for the four and a half months he spent doing time for "some mob-action shit." That's what he'd called it when I asked him why he had to go to court. He'd assured me, his girlfriend of just a few months, that the whole group-aggravated-battery thing was a simple matter of wrong place, wrong time, as if the cops had only pinned something on him because of his previous record. When we'd met the summer before, he seemed like a regular, appealingly dangerous seventeen-year-old boy.

On a Saturday in the spring of my junior year in high school, I accompanied Tammy on the hour and a half drive up to the prison where Jack was being held. He would be there until a spot opened up in boot camp, a military-style training program—also known as "shock incarceration"—intended to shorten sentences for non-serial offenders. Tammy and I had gone to the mall the weekend before, where she handed me a hundred dollar bill to buy Jack an all-white pair of Nikes that would pass the boot camp's regulations. When the sales associate at Finish Line tried to show me other options, and I explained why I needed the all-white ones, his eyes bulged as if they were trying to escape his head, and he turned to get me the size thirteens.

Tammy and I smoked cigarettes the whole way to Joliet Correctional Facility, which has since been shuttered and used as the fictional Fox River prison on television. When I watched the show *Prison Break* several years later, I couldn't figure out why I found the medieval-style limestone building, complete with turrets, so triggering. I'd conveniently forgotten the time I was a visitor.

As we approached the barbed-wire fence, I asked Tammy what kinds of criminals were locked up inside. "They got murderers and rapists," she said, pulling over to dump the joint roaches out of her ashtray. "All kinds of shit." I noticed that, along with the Nikes, she had brought a brown paper bag full of magazines and peeked through them when we stopped for gas. Some were about cars but most were pornography: naked blonde women with their legs spread open, sprawled out on top of cars or squatting next to motorcycles.

Once we got inside, past the metal detector, I heard whistles and catcalls. I kept my eyes focused straight ahead. It had been difficult to choose an outfit that morning. I wanted to look sexy for my prison boyfriend but hadn't fully considered the murderers and rapists. Suddenly I was hyper-aware of my cleavage, showcased by the neckline of my favorite nautical navy-blue spandex camisole. I zipped up my jacket.

When we entered the small, plain visitation room, furnished with a few four-seat tables and vending machines, Jack was already there, waiting. He was wearing what could have been white hospital scrubs, if you ignored the numbers across the back, and he looked pale, like he'd just seen his first spleen—his green eyes were vivid against the sallow backdrop of his skin. I hugged his six-foot-three frame as Tammy went to buy us snacks from the vending machine. Except for that initial greeting, we weren't allowed to touch at all. He seemed shaken by his new surroundings, but not afraid. I knew I didn't have to worry about him, but something in me shifted when I saw he couldn't be the protective, affectionate boyfriend I had fallen for in the first place.

Twenty years later, our short visit is a blur. More memorable is the joint Tammy and I shared on the way home. After seeing her 220-pound adult baby in prison, she was uncharacteristically silent. Typically, she would ramble on about her boyfriend or her neighbors, who were always doing something that bugged her. "That's ate up," she'd quip, her shaggy bleached-blonde hair pulled half-up and held in place with a scrunchie, her long bangs swaying back and forth as she shook her head.

With Jack temporarily out of the picture, I was spending more time with Tammy. I'd come over, and she'd sit in a rocking chair, yakking on about nonsense and every so often getting up to look out the window, as if something important, or threatening, might be happening out there.

"I hear that," I'd respond after almost everything she said, waiting for her to catch on that I had no clue what she was talking about. She never did. Unlike my own mother, who criticized how I dressed and acted, Tammy couldn't have cared less about how I presented myself. Her overly tan face was covered in wrinkles, though she couldn't have been more than forty. She wore crop tops that revealed a leathery stomach—and a belly button that sank into her petite frame like the mouth of a rotting pumpkin during an unseasonably warm October.

My hometown is an unremarkable stop off Interstate 55, which cuts a path between Chicago and Saint Louis through soybean and corn fields. Not only was there nothing to do there growing up, but there was no nearby city that felt worth aspiring to—and before the internet, no real connection to the outside world. I was sheltered, unaware that the privileges I enjoyed as a member of the upper middle class were not universal. My parents were quite strict, and in response, I became rebellious. Every one of their actions had an equal and opposite reaction. They grounded me for drinking; I snuck out. They threw away my cigarettes; I pulled them out of the trash. They flushed my weed; I stole twenties from my father's wallet to replace it.

This went on until I somehow broke them; they gave up, and we mostly stopped speaking. But they let me keep driving their Honda as long as I kept my grades up and got a job every summer. At sixteen, I worked as a lifeguard at a public park, collecting cash for paddleboat rentals and ensuring that patrons were equipped with life jackets. Because I was a pothead, I skimmed off the paddleboat operation to order myself deliveries, which came in through a chain-link fence behind the shed where I was stationed.

When my weed dealer told me about a party on the college campus in my town, I went. There I met seventeen-year-old Jack. Almost two years older than me, he was ruggedly handsome in a white V-neck T-shirt and jeans. He didn't say much but somehow managed to command the kind of respect normally reserved for star athletes or mob bosses.

I noticed our hair was the same color—light brown with highlights. I later learned he'd put a garbage bag on his head, poked holes in it, and bleached whatever bits of hair he could pull through. The appropriate terminology for the result—popular in 1998—was "frosted tips." I bleached my hair yellow straight from a bottle since my mother wouldn't pay for me to have it done professionally.

At the party, the boys drank beer in the flatbed of Jack's blue pickup. Jack looked at me intently, his green eyes picking up on my insecurity. "You're pretty," he said, lighting my cigarette. I noticed a fresh scar on his hand, and he told me he had just gotten out of jail. He explained he'd gotten drunk and punched through a front-door window—the cause of both the scar and his arrest.

He was unconcerned with sports, popularity, and high school society in general—things I also hated, but for different reasons. I was too rebellious for the nerds, too smart for the jocks, and not into drama class. I didn't fit in anywhere, so I smoked pot constantly to temper my social anxiety. He drank heavily, gambled over card games at his mom's trailer, and rode shotgun in my car while eating pork rinds—a snack I hadn't even known existed. (After Jack got locked up, I found a lone pork rind between the passenger seat and the door—and cried.)

By the fall of my junior year, Jack and I had become a couple, and he took me to homecoming. We doubled with my best friend, Alex, and her boyfriend, the star of the football team. Jack seemed uncomfortable when he showed up at my parents' house—a white-brick home on a maple-lined boulevard—in dress slacks and a button-up shirt. I wore a royal-blue satin dress. My parents took photos of us before we went to the only fancy hotel restaurant in town to get burgers.

After dinner, while traveling to the dance in the football star's jeep, the air thick with the scent of our rose corsages, another driver motioned angrily at us for cutting him off. Jack rolled down his window, made a deep Marlboro-Red-infused gurgle, and launched the largest loogie I'd ever seen. It sailed over the lane marker and directly onto the other driver's side window. The man—in his mid-thirties, likely, and wearing glasses—looked back at us from behind the yellow slime, horrified. We all hesitated before breaking into laughter.

I was making a habit of skipping school to hang out with Tammy, chiming in on her rants just so I had someone amusing to get stoned with. Jack didn't smoke pot, and his relationship with his mom mostly consisted of good-natured ribbing, although sometimes Tammy would get fed up with his antics and let out her equivalent of a sigh—a long, deep, exaggerated *Jeeee-sus*. She was the kind of mother who, at the time, seemed novel—less like a parent and more like a cool older sister, which meant she let us have sex at her place.

That November, I got pregnant. I didn't bother to tell Tammy and hid it from my own parents, along with the abortion I quickly decided to have. Jack drove me almost two hours away to the nearest clinic in Illinois, where protesters carried signs about killing babies and screamed at the car as we entered the parking lot.

"Bunch of assholes," Jack said.

He walked me inside, and once my name was called, waited in the parking lot. When I came back out dazed, the sunlight burning my eyes, I spotted the smoke from his Marlboros rising up from the sunroof of my teal '95 Honda Accord. I felt sick but not sad. Just a few weeks later, Jack committed the crime that would send him to Fox River—his "mob action shit"—and the following month he received his five-month sentence.

Once he was gone, I'd go over to Tammy's house on Sunday nights and talk to Jack, who could call collect only once a week. Sometimes I'd get to answer the phone and hear the recording: *You have a collect call from*—he'd say his full name—*at Joliet Correctional Facility*. He also sent letters to my home address, which my mother collected and read before eventually handing them over in a screening process that seemed, to me, at least as strict as the prison's.

"I don't know why I'm letting you have these," she sighed, raising an eyebrow. "Some interesting illustrations in there."

She had not expected to find teddy bears, drawn by a convicted felon, on an envelope addressed to her teenage daughter. I thought they expressed his soft interior, hidden from the rest of the world but accessible to me. The lines had been traced over so many times the pen had nearly punctured the paper— the same ink, I later learned, he'd also used to give himself a prison tat, a small blue mark at the base of his thumb. Happy to have proof he'd been thinking about me, I looked past his misspelled declarations of love and toward the promises he made about getting his life straightened out.

He became my first long-distance boyfriend. At seventeen, the relationship that existed within the confines of my own head satisfied teenage social pressures to have a significant other, as well as my penchant for melodrama: I loved someone, and we'd been torn apart by a force greater than my parents. All of this made me believe in starry-eyed things like destiny and romance, while, in reality, Jack and I didn't know each other all that well. We'd only been together for six months and hadn't had a real fight.

With Jack gone, I was free to hang out every night at the apartment the boys in the graduating class above me had rented for the summer—or "The A-P-T," as we called it. My friends and I would go there and smoke weed in an outdoor stairwell overlooking the train tracks, talk about *The Blair Witch Project* and shriek, while the boys sat there squinting, red-eyed from smoking.

I found myself attracted to one of them and ended up going home with him. We agreed that no one should know, especially not Jack. When I went to his house I would park in a lot down the street, and he would look both ways out the front door before letting me in. But I couldn't help myself and eventually confessed the affair to a friend, who, predictably, told Jack's ex-girlfriend. If I had learned anything from hours of watching Jerry Springer after school, it should have been to keep my fool mouth shut.

When I Google Jack today, I find, on the first page of the search results, his MySpace page, a 2005 mug shot (from when he was charged with resisting arrest while on parole, shortly after getting out of prison following another sentence, years after I knew him) and a court document referencing an abusive relationship. In a public database, I also find records of at least twenty criminal charges, nine of which include a form of battery. When I see the word "domestic" in front of one, I begin to sweat.

I'd tried to block out how our relationship ended, to move on. But even with years of therapy, it was difficult—partly because I wasn't sure about exactly what had happened. It took me two decades of living 900 miles away to build up the courage to request copies of the court documents from my case. They arrived at my apartment in New York City, where I worked for a women's fashion brand. My days were spent reviewing photography layouts featuring stick-thin models in oversized minimalist garb, their eyes vacant.

When I emptied the contents of the manila envelope onto my marble tabletop, some of what I found surprised me: the fact that, the year we broke up, Jack had been charged a $100 domestic violence fine and then been processed through court collections for not paying it. Or that I still recognized the backward slant of his handwriting on one of the forms—and could imagine the tip of his tongue sticking out through the side of his teeth as he carefully printed each tiny letter of his name. But mostly, I was surprised at the acts described in the charging documents.

Jack and I remained a couple for the duration of his sentence. At his boot camp graduation, he looked proud, an expression so unfamiliar it read almost like a mask. He was happy to see me, and standing there looking at him—in uniform and boots, with his conservative haircut, marching in formation—I believed things could be different. But once he returned to a less structured life, his temper flared back up and his fledgling ambitions dimmed. With a criminal record and without a high school diploma, he couldn't do much but work for his dad's appliance company while sorting out his GED.

For the rest of the summer, he drank heavily and seemed even rowdier than he had before he left. At first, I liked having him back and relished the familiar scent of his Drakkar Noir cologne. But I began to miss my independence.

While I was at school, Jack started hanging out with two girls who had already graduated. One was tall and standoffish, with a permanent glower. The other was short, squat, and heavily made-up. I suspected he was sleeping with at least one of them. When I asked him about it, he said I was being ridiculous. I didn't push it. Instead, I avoided the issue altogether and kept seeing the other guy secretly—until Jack called to confront me.

"I saw your car there," he said.

"No, you didn't," I replied, praying he'd been too drunk to read my plates.

He seemed to accept my explanation and let it go. But the next time I arrived at his house for a party, I was faced with hostility. The two blondes stood in the kitchen holding beers to their lips, the tall one giving me her signature glare from under a gray beanie. I walked back outside to smoke a cigarette. Jack followed me out. He seemed drunk. The dark night hung heavy over our heads.

"Where have you been?" he asked.

Then came the part I didn't remember until I read through the court file: he grabbed me by the shoulders and shook me—hard. In the memory that flashed in my head when I looked at the documents, his face is grainy, as if captured on black-and-white film in low light. My insides are the liquid sloshing around in a glass before it spills, at gravity's mercy as I wait for the teetering to end.

The next part, though, I've always remembered, in slow motion.

He stopped shaking me, drew back his arm, and punched me square in the jaw. My reaction felt cartoon-like: I saw stars, and then everything went white. The impact knocked me backward, but I didn't have time to be stunned because the pain set in so fast that I just clutched my head and wobbled toward the door to the house, yelling inside for my friend Alex. When she got outside, Jack was gone.

I handed her my keys, but she didn't know how to drive stick. The guy she was with did, but he was fifteen and only had a learner's permit. I told him to get in and drive anyway. As he adjusted the driver's seat, I sat in the back holding my throbbing forehead. I could barely think. But instinct told me to get out of there as quickly as possible.

This is where my memory goes blank again.

After reading the charges, which included criminal trespass to a vehicle,

I remembered Jack banging on the driver's side window. In the driver's seat, Alex's date, who didn't know what had just taken place, rolled it partway down. "You better let me in," Jack said, reaching his large forearm through the crack, fumbling around for the lock to let himself in—*so he can drag me back out* I now remember thinking.

As the driver rolled up the window and shifted us into reverse, Jack disappeared again. And then suddenly he was back—he ran at the car and punched the windshield, his fist resounding with a loud *thump* as it cracked but didn't shatter. We'd finally backed out and shifted into drive, but Jack was chasing us. As the car picked up speed, he threw his half-full can of Budweiser; it bounced off the bumper and made a *thunk* before landing in the street. Had he been holding his beer the entire time—or just taking sips between blows?

The next morning, I woke up with a throbbing headache and a split lip. I washed the dried blood off and examined my face in the mirror. I didn't feel like the victim of an assault; I felt like the victim of a particularly brutal dumping. My eyes were puffy from crying, and my cheek was slightly bruised. I looked ugly, pathetic—disposable, even. I hoped my parents wouldn't notice my face, but I would have to tell them about their car.

When I came downstairs, my mother was sitting at the kitchen table.

"I need to show you something," I said, my voice wavering.

I started to cry as I led her out to the garage, my father following. No one said anything about my injuries, but I had the distinct feeling that I was in trouble—or, at the very least, had somehow brought this upon myself.

I drove the car to the police station, peering through the largest shards in my cracked windshield, as my mother trailed me in her Toyota Avalon. The detective who took my statement was wearing a blue suit and looked like half of a police duo from a television show, though she also reminded me of Hillary Clinton, who at the time had short, feathered strawberry blonde hair. I asked if I could choose whether to press charges, and she told me I could not. The story I wanted to tell myself—that maybe Jack didn't deserve to go back to jail over his cheating girlfriend—slipped away in her presence. Once the state had been presented with evidence of domestic violence, they proceeded with charges themselves. All I had to do was show up for court, and Jack would be forced to plead guilty.

A couple weeks later, I heard through a friend that Jack wanted to talk— he wanted to apologize but was afraid of the restraining order. I agreed to meet him, looking for some explanation that would absolve me of any responsibility for his fate. I knew Jack's father had been violent when he was growing up and even heard he'd put Tammy in the hospital once. She'd told me about it herself. But I never wondered what she could have done to deserve it.

Jack appeared sober and serious when we sat in his blue truck, parked in an alley on a sunny day. He looked at the floor and cried, his face red with shame. He sounded genuine when he apologized, and for a moment, I pitied him. There was something tender about this, the two of us intimately connected through violence. But the conversation quickly turned to practical matters.

"I could get seven years," he said and mentioned that charges would be dropped if I didn't show up for court.

"It's too late," I told him. Other witnesses had already given statements, and my parents weren't going to let the vandalism of their car slide. Part of me was glad the case didn't hinge on my testimony.

The court date wasn't for another several months, and in January I moved into a single dorm room and started college early at the university in my town. I felt out of place there and didn't go to class or mingle with the other students. Like a frightened squirrel escaping a predator, I flung myself at the nearest branch without thinking about whether it was a suitable place to land. My new boyfriend worked at a car wash and shared my affinity for MDMA.

He and I lay in my bed one late night after a rave, covered in cold sweat, when I heard the sharp click of the metal lock on my door. The door opened a crack and then quickly closed. Had we left it unlocked, and had some drunk person stumbled into the wrong dorm room? My boyfriend jumped up and looked out into the hall before quickly slamming the door and hitting the deadbolt. His eyes were wide.

Jack was pacing the halls. He'd gotten past the sign-in desk and picked the lock with a credit card before realizing I wasn't alone. After beating his fists on the door, he eventually left through an emergency exit, which locked behind him. He yelled at us from outside until campus police came and he fled the scene.

When I showed up to the courthouse as a witness in the state's case, I wasn't expecting to find Jack's girlfriend standing in the hallway next to Tammy. But there she was—a striking brunette with a deep tan and long hair. Her eyes trailed me as I walked by, her expression cold. It's pretty outrageous to bring your new squeeze to the court date where you'll need to cop to battering your old squeeze, but that didn't even cross my mind. Somehow I still loved him. We make sense of violent events by choosing to deny that they happened—or by blaming the victim. This is true even if the victim is yourself.

After Jack entered his guilty plea, my mother, my friend Alex, and I left the courthouse and walked toward the car. That's when we heard Tammy yell.

"I'm gonna kill you, bitch."

From across the parking lot, I could see the lines in her face deepening into a scowl. Too stunned to process her threat, I watched as the brunette climbed into her black truck to occupy what had once been my seat.

What happened when I was seventeen never really left me. It surfaced from my subconscious periodically, sometimes unexpectedly, only to recede again once I recognized it. In the years that followed, I had a recurring nightmare in which Jack chased me around with a gun. In my twenties, every night I spent alone I'd hear the imaginary click of a lock being picked. In my thirties, I'd catch glimpses of his figure in the outlines of any men who happened to be walking toward me at dusk.

Forgetting turned out to be impossible, so, eventually, I chose to remember instead. When I emailed the state's attorney for more information twenty years after the fact, I asked for any and all available documents—whatever I was entitled to as the victim in the case. I realized I didn't even know how much time Jack had served.

I feel unresolved, I wrote.

The attorney responded that the judge had recommended a misdemeanor domestic battery charge, which carried a maximum of one year in jail. But because he was already on probation for a felony, he received a two-and-a-half-year sentence and likely served only half.

It was a far cry from seven years.

Encouraged, I dug deeper. From newspaper clippings, I was able to find out the real reason Jack had been in jail the summer before we started dating: he served seventy-eight days for a violent home invasion. He had punched through a window in order to break, enter, and attack the man who lived there.

In the county court's database, I discovered further details about his nine recorded battery charges. Five specified "physical contact," which is what differentiates battery from assault, and three took it a step further, noting either "bodily harm" or "injury." The one that sent him to Fox River was described as "aggravated," which implies more severe injuries.

None of his victims were named. But I saw myself hiding in the letters that made up the phrase "bodily harm" like a scared animal in sparse grass.

On and off for years, I had thought about the homecoming photo my parents took of Jack and me, the only picture I had of us together. I'd avoided looking at it. After I read the court documents, I rifled through boxes until I found it.

In the photo, I look so happy next to Jack, in my royal-blue satin gown with sequins across the bust. My hair is pulled up into a fancy bun, and a few blonde tendrils frame my face. Jack's frosted tips have grown out. He looks like the guy I fell for. He looks like trouble. He looks like a seventeen-year-old boy.

THE DIVING WELL

We stood in line behind the diving board, our blonde-haired legs touching at the knees and ankles, hands clasped across our red Speedo racing suits as we waited our turns at acrobatic feats. Each time I entered the cool water, I would swim downward, my ears popping as I approached the drain, before suddenly realizing my oxygen was running out. A prickle of fear sent my little body kicking back to the surface.

During the long, hot summer days, almost as far back as I can remember, my best friend Natalie and I went to swim practice in the mornings, ate grilled cheese sandwiches for lunch, and then spent the afternoons flying into—and climbing out of—a square pool known as the diving well. Every August, I'd return to school, my light hair tinged green from soaking all summer in chlorinated waters.

Natalie was my first friend. My mother worked as a physical therapist in her father's sports medicine clinic. As babies, we were due around the same date but born three weeks apart. She showed up early, and I arrived two weeks late.

We grew up in a suburb smack in the middle of Illinois without any real urban anchor to tether its floating inhabitants. The *Nancy Drew* books I acquired bi-weekly from our local library lasted only a few hours—my own primitive form of binge entertainment. My parents decided to join the same country club that Natalie's parents had when they learned it would keep their kids occupied during the months off from school. While our adult counterparts played tennis or golf or drank Arnold Palmers, Natalie and I spent hours at the pool.

"You're not going to just sit around the house all day," my mother would say on the weekends when we didn't have swim practice. She'd round up my swimming gear and tell me to call Natalie so we could pick her up on the way. She'd then drop us off in the pool parking lot, sometimes without shoes, the asphalt burning the soles of our feet. We'd waddle through the front gate, towels around our waists, ready to meet whatever adventures awaited us.

A regular, or "big pool," as we called it, stretched between the diving boards and tennis courts. The big pool was painted royal blue and offered only measly depths of nine feet. We swam laps back and forth in its monotonous lanes during morning swim practice and then took a splash in the two-foot baby pool, which had been painted white and separated from the others by a chain-link fence. Natalie and I agreed that because it was so warm and shallow, it was likely filled with pee, which became a self-fulfilling prophecy.

But the diving well was by far our favorite amenity, save for maybe the snack bar. Painted the pale blue of an Easter egg, the well boasted depths of fourteen feet. It was also surrounded by chain link, and it required its own lifeguard. If Natalie and I showed up to find it empty, a teenager in a red swimsuit—complete with a white cross—would sulk toward it with the key, giving up a nap in the guard room to make sure neither of us was gravely injured on his or her watch. Natalie and I could out-maneuver most people in the diving well. If it was already in use when we arrived, we would shame away the cannon-ballers by showing off our high skill and stamina.

"Check this out," Natalie would say before flying off the high dive, grabbing her leg behind her back with one arm and placing the other behind her head, as if she were posing for a photo mid-air.

"Better?" I'd ask after executing the same back dive six or seven times off the one-meter springboard. I enjoyed practicing my list of dives for upcoming swim meets, where I collected blue ribbon after blue ribbon. The diving well was the only place that I found discipline comforting as a child.

It was also a place where we pulled pranks on each other—an extra boost on the board from behind as we were jumping off, or a smack from one of those super-absorbent mini sports towels.

It was a place where bodies—large and small—went *splat*, where "oohs" and "ahs" rose from the crowds that had gathered to watch the performance.

People especially loved to see Natalie. Even as a little girl, she was solid muscle, a masculine kind of beauty with thick blonde hair. She was also a fearless diver who would belly flop off the high dive for props alone or complete as many flips as possible before smacking the water wherever she happened to be in rotation. She'd then emerge, her face frozen in an open-mouthed smile, her expression half-covered by strands of wet hair, which had long since refused to be tamed by any ponytail holder.

Natalie and I were about the same size, but I was lankier, having inherited my mother's form—including dainty lower legs and toes that pointed nicely.

My strength was finesse. Because I was deathly afraid of heights, I lingered on the one-meter perfecting simple dives: a flip with a twist and an inward, which requires you to jump off backward and then dive forward, entering the water head-first.

My mother had also been a diver growing up and would sit for hours in a chair under a tree giving me tips. I'd see her there every time I emerged from the depths. "You're leaning back too much on your approach," she'd say to explain the less-than-perfect entry on my back dive.

I was trying to avoid knocking my heels on the board, which had happened once before. The real dangers of swimming hadn't even registered as a possibility in my mind. I knew we weren't supposed to run, horse around on the ladders, or leave the gates open, but I didn't fully understand why—until one afternoon.

A little boy had been with his mother in the locker room before wandering out past the baby pool and into the diving well. No one saw him floating facedown at the other end until our swim team coach, standing on the three-meter, dove in to rescue him. The coach handed the toddler out to my mother, who was certified in CPR, and as he went to call an ambulance, my mother used two fingers to do compressions on the boy's sternum. His lungs had filled with water, so she turned him on his side before the lifeguards and then the paramedics took over.

The boy survived but something had irrevocably changed. Suddenly the diving well was no longer a source of delighted shrieks but more like the cold, sterile hole in the ground it appeared to be when we drove by in the winter.

The summer after sixth grade, Natalie and I went to diving camp at Indiana University—just three hours east of our hometown in Illinois. The college was known for its Olympic-grade facilities and top athletic program, and we were its youngest recruits—too young, even, to make use of our newfound freedom alone in the dorms. Instead, we trained constantly for the two weeks we spent there—at the pool, in weight rooms, and even outdoors.

My favorite activity involved a trampoline with a harness. It combined fun with safety, allowing you to isolate parts of dives that are simply not important enough to your survival mid-air to be able to think closely about them. I worked a lot on my twists. One of my best was a back dive with one and a half somersaults and one and a half twists. The dive was tricky—it required a sequence of arm and body movements to happen at split-second intervals. Drop your arm but not your head and you wouldn't get enough spin. Start your twist too early and kill your vertical rotation. To experiment with timing and form in the pool, you'd have to be a masochist who enjoys climbing out of the water over and over with thighs bright red and smarting from smacking full-force against the surface. Instead, I did it twenty times in a harness.

"Now you're getting it," the coach told me.

I beamed—a twelve-year-old girl being trained by a college coach. Diving had, by process of elimination, become the sport of my dreams. It was the only thing I was *really* good at. I thought for sure I would dive my way to collegiate greatness.

"Whoa, there," I heard him say after I finished my time on the trampoline. Natalie was supposed to do two flips in the harness but had rotated almost four times instead. We weren't particularly competitive with one another—our strengths and tastes were so different that it was almost a surprise we were good friends at all.

To fill in where I lacked, Natalie had male friends. In fact, she'd buddied up with one of the guys at camp. He was an eighth-grader and a daredevil himself. The rumor was they'd made out in a grassy field one night and he might have "gone down her pants." I didn't really know what this entailed—Natalie wasn't the type to kiss and tell—but it sounded dangerous and so it made sense that she would be testing it out first.

I still had my girlhood crush on Greg Louganis, who was, at the time, the best diver in the world. He was long and lean and filled out his Speedo in a non-threatening but curious way. He'd also just come out to the world as gay and HIV-positive. The divers at camp all discussed how, when he'd hit his head during the 1988 Olympics six years before and bled into the pool, Louganis had failed to tell anyone about the status of his disease. With only ten minutes before his next dive, the on-site Olympic doctor had stitched up his wound without gloves. This was during the height of the AIDS panic in the early '90s, which basically equated unprotected sex with death.

"He should have told his doctor," Natalie said in the matter-of-fact way that junior high kids say things they don't know anything about.

I nodded because I'd recently watched a video in health class titled

"Blood-borne Pathogens," which explained how a virus could live for multiple days on a dry surface. The same class had briefly touched on abstinence as a form of protection.

To have one foot in childhood and another in adolescence is truly terrifying. You know *of* things but not about them. I hadn't yet had any talks with my mother about sex—I only knew that I wasn't supposed to do it. Sexuality had been spun to me as some sort of external lurking force waiting to corrupt children. It was my responsibility to occupy myself with "wholesome" activities like sports, which required discipline and a kind of vigilant self-guardianship, but sustained mastery over one's body is nearly impossible. I couldn't dive forever.

At camp every night after dinner, we cut across a field of yellow grass in our flip-flops, our swimsuits under our clothes, towels draped over our shoulders like togas, and headed toward the outdoor pool for the five-, seven-, and ten-meter platforms.

Part of camp tradition was to launch a dive off the highest platform during the first week. I begrudgingly followed Natalie up the slippery black metal ladder, trying not to look down. As a competitive event, platform diving is literally called "tower," and the three-meter diving board I'd always avoided at home now seemed puny by comparison.

As we passed the five-meter platform, time seemed to slow to a crawl. Rung by rung, we climbed higher and higher, past the seven-meter, as the people on the deck got smaller and smaller. At dusk from the top, a few stories up, the water in this unfamiliar ultra-deep diving well reflected the sepia tint of the brown concrete structure.

"If you land flat, the impact can break your back," one of the older divers told us.

I tried to hide my internal panic. As I debated what would happen if the fire department had to come get me, Natalie ran by me on the platform, impulsively throwing herself into a dive with multiple flips before entering the water, her arms outstretched above her head. How she intuited precisely how much to rotate from a ten-meter platform escapes me still. I didn't have to see her face to know she came up smiling.

"C'mon, Sarah," I could hear her yell from below.

I inched to the front of the platform, which was covered in black rubber tread and droplets of water.

Once, as a little girl, I'd followed Natalie up to the rafters in her family's tool shed to play clubhouse and then cried because I was afraid. Her mom had to come out with a ladder to get me down. I had probably only been nine feet up.

This time, I was thirty-three feet up, and no one was coming for me. I couldn't simply jump because the drop was so far that I knew I'd rotate forward and end up smacking my face. Crawling back down the slippery ladder seemed equally treacherous. The only way off was to dive. Since I had no other choice, I let the platform slip away from my toes and reached for the hazy, yolk-orange horizon. I held my body as tightly as possible, squeezing my hands together above my head. The drop was disturbingly long. When my hands finally broke the surface, I could feel my shoulder blades and back scrape the water behind me. It was like trying to penetrate concrete. When I re-emerged, I could hear Natalie cheering.

"I knew you could do it," she said, before heading back up the ladder.

Never again, I thought, shivering. I rested one elbow over the side of the pool as the water lapped past it and into the drain. I hadn't conquered my fear; I'd just suspended it momentarily.

When we were sophomores in high school, the same coach from Indiana University used our town's indoor college pool once a week to coach possible recruits. He was much tougher on us than I'd remembered.

At camp three and a half years earlier, I'd learned a dive that I had never been able to grasp on my own: the reverse. To do it, you have to jump off forward and then dive backward, aiming your head back toward the springboard. In order to land an almost vertical entry and get a good score, you're also required to stay relatively close to the board. This presents an inherent danger with any dive, but because the reverse is blind, it's a literal leap of faith. Not only do you have to trust your own body, challenging enough for any teenage girl, but also the physics of a springboard, which is engineered to throw you out.

The farther you lean away from the board out of fear, the more difficult it is to initiate a backward rotation.

Don't throw yourself out enough, and you'll end up like Greg Louganis in the qualifying round of the 1988 Olympics. He was attempting a reverse two-and-a-half, his body folded flat in half—the pike position. As he opened back up after two rotations to prepare for entry, the crown of his skull hit the board.

At diving camp, I'd learned the simplest version of the reverse, a dive, which I did while wearing a safety harness that resembled a chastity belt. In the years since, I'd upgraded it to a reverse one-and-a-half, tucked into a ball. But because diving is scored by a combination of how difficult a dive is and how well you execute it, once you perfect your list, you can only up your score potential by continually learning new dives with higher numerical degrees of difficulty.

Now, on our second week of practice with the Indiana University coach, he tried to help us do just that.

"I want to see a reverse one-and-a-half, in the pike position," the coach commanded. It was significantly harder than rotating in a ball, as I'd practiced. In fact, I was pretty sure it would be impossible. For me anyway.

"Off the three-meter," he clarified.

For the fearless, attempting this dive from higher up actually made it more feasible—you have more time to rotate. Natalie delivered on the request in about twenty seconds, although it resulted in a rather large splash. I declined altogether.

"If you can't get past your fear, then I don't see the point in you being here," the coach told me.

My heart hit the bottom of my stomach and sat there like a clump of debris that had gathered on a drain, waiting to be collected by a pool skimmer.

I couldn't do it; I was too scared. But the threat of failure loomed even larger. Failing my coach. Failing Natalie. Failing my mother, who sat dutifully in the stands. I had no idea being good at something would come with such pressure to always be better.

The following week, I climbed straight up the ladder to the three-meter springboard. Dark blue waves lapped between the red and white lane markers of the Olympic-sized "big pool" stretching in front of me beyond a bridge of tile. White caps bobbed silently down and back in the lanes as bent arms sliced through the surface.

I took a deep breath and somehow managed to block it all out: my fear of heights, of slipping on the board, of splitting my head open. All of these fates seemed better than running crying into the locker room. But when I successfully completed the dive, I felt exactly the same way I had after diving off the ten-meter platform at camp—proud, relieved, and terrified that someone would make me do it again.

"There you go!" said the coach.

This time, I did not beam. I knew I couldn't keep it up.

There is a concept for failure in diving called a "no dive," which is essentially equivalent to a zero. No matter how hideous your entry, if you fulfill the necessary rotations and positioning, even if you go in kicking and screaming, you'll get at least half of a point. If you are unable to complete—or even attempt—the dive, you do not receive a score.

In the end, at fifteen, I took the "no dive." I didn't go back to the indoor pool with its delicate balance of warm, humid air and cool, chlorinated waters. When it demanded more from me than I was able to give, I quit altogether.

I turned toward other ways to fill a widening gap of unmet expectations—from my parents, teachers, peers. A nicotine addiction to distract from my AP-level homework, which just kept getting harder. A marijuana habit to dull the constant sting of not being skinny or pretty enough. Drunk sex with boys I didn't even like. Instead of a clear focus on achievement, I settled for the muddled avoidance of my own humiliation.

Natalie stopped diving that same year to focus on other sports. We still hung out often, finding ourselves engaged in activities that required little verbal communication. We'd become used to our silent partnership at the pool, where a shake of the head, a laugh, or a thumbs-up said everything. At sixteen, we hit the ski slopes together—Natalie taking long jumps on her snowboard and me trying to keep my skis properly paralleled through the maze of icy moguls. At seventeen, I got into her car on a Friday after school, and she unloaded her bra to reveal a bag of psychedelic mushrooms. We went back to her house and ate them on pizza before going to the mall, where I froze in panic, *because how the hell are we going to park between all of these cars?* Of course, Natalie was in the driver's seat and nailed a perpendicular entry into a parking space on the first try.

Our senior year in high school, Natalie moved to Orlando to become a semi-pro wakeboarder. She eventually injured her knee, moved, and switched sports again—this time to row crew at Berkeley. I stayed closer to home, attending the University of Illinois the following year. I lived in a dorm right across the street from the campus recreation center. When the weather was warm, I would lounge at the outdoor pool and look longingly toward the water. Sometimes I'd see the women's swim team leaving in athletic warm-ups, their hair still wet from morning practice.

It wasn't the activity itself that I missed but the sense of camaraderie, the joyful release of energy, and the utter exhaustion I'd once felt after diving my heart out. I knew I could never have my sport—or my friend—back the way things had once been. Even though college offered exciting new experiences, part of me preferred the familiar lull of childhood to the uncharted waters of life as an adult.

Some people thrive off the adrenaline rush that comes with danger. I, on the other hand, would have stayed in the light blue diving well forever.

BEFORE EMPOWERMENT

His brown eyes trailed over my body in an exaggerated way. It could have been considered sexual harassment, had it happened at work. But at the bar, and uninhibited, I felt the rush of being seen.

At twenty-two, I was lonely and working in a restaurant. Nic was a server I had a crush on who'd hardly ever spoken to me until we bumped into each other on a random night off. He walked into a Chicago dive bar where I happened to be getting drunk with a friend. I approached him from behind to order myself another round.

"Corona—with a lemon," I said to the bartender. Somehow I'd gotten the impression that this was the sophisticated European way to drink cheap beer. I left a dollar and change on the bar before forcing my lemon wedge into the bottle, ready to make my move.

"Hi, Nic," I said to the half-moon formed by the adjustable snaps on the back of his hat. The half-moon turned. Nic set his Heineken down before slowly looking me up and down. He seemed to still be processing my identity.

Perhaps it was my off-duty attire that threw him. During shifts behind the restaurant bar, I was forced to wear black button-up shirts and dress pants, my shoulder-length hair in a ponytail. That evening, I donned a dive-bar appropriate denim and pink tank top combo. My long bangs were swept to one side, my light hair down.

"Sa-rah," he finally answered, his mouth widening into a smile. The slow, deliberate way he lingered over both syllables of my name made it seem as if he knew something about me that I didn't, or at least not yet.

Instead of being offended by the once-over, I was awash in a familiar response—pleasure mixed with shame. Sexual objectification can trigger conflicting impulses. On the one hand, I wanted to be treated with respect. On the other hand, I wanted to be wanted.

In 2004, I had recently graduated college and broken up with my long-term boyfriend while on study abroad in Rome—mostly so I could ride around on the back of an Italian guy's Vespa, guilt-free. After returning stateside, I got a job at a tapas bar while interning at a museum downtown. When I told people where I worked, they always heard "a topless bar," and I'd have to explain I did not peddle bacon-wrapped dates while wearing health-code mandated pasties. Instead, I dressed like a Subway sandwich artist, doling out mojitos and spicy potatoes that were covered in mayonnaise and dotted with red flakes.

I met Nic at the restaurant. In his late twenties, he had dark features, a wide smile, and one of those near-silent laughs where his head moved but not much sound came out. At work, we never spoke or even exchanged glances. He didn't pay any attention to me. I can't say when or why it happened, only that somehow, I developed a crush on him.

"I have nice teeth," he would later tell me, running his tongue along the smooth edges of his pearly white incisors, as if this mere fact were an answer to everything. As if I'd come to him looking for an answer to anything.

A few weeks after I saw him outside of work, we ran into each other again—this time at a bar in Wicker Park. It was the kind of place you go last. Reps from R.J. Reynolds were always there giving away free cigarettes; their electronic ID checkers offered the only lights in a nearly pitch-black room. I'd once been thrown out of the place for having a food fight with my roommate and knocking her off the barstool.

When I arrived, I saw Nic in a corner laughing with some of the other servers from our restaurant. I didn't waste too much time with small talk.

"Got any weed?" I asked him.

"At my apartment," he said, smiling.

When we got to his house, I engaged in the formality of smoking a bowl before he generously offered me a place to crash: his bed.

"I won't even touch you," he said.

I stripped down to my white underwear and bra before making myself comfortable. He turned off the lights, which made what we were about to do seem like a covert operation, in which we both knew the mission but hadn't yet discussed ground strategy. I could feel him tentatively crossing from his side of the mattress over to mine. Eventually, he slung his arm across my hip and moved his head toward me.

His kiss felt natural on my lips—like it had been there all along.

The next morning, I started what would become a familiar ritual of ripping the manila envelope and yellow ticket off of my windshield, cringing at the $100 fine, and then consoling myself with a cigarette. Slow, deliberate circling for free parking at night in a crowded neighborhood of Chicago required the kind of patience not found in someone who sensed sex on the horizon. So I'd park at a meter and tell myself I'd get up and leave before the meter maid came. Instead, I came and didn't want to leave.

At work, Nic still barely acknowledged my existence. I read this not so much as a slight toward me as an indication of the fact that he wasn't technically available. I'd heard from other employees he was in a protracted breakup with his girlfriend. The details weren't exactly clear—nor did I exactly care.

I'd go out with my friends and then, around midnight, text him from my shitty Motorola flip phone to see if he was home. I'd stay overnight at his place, accepting that I'd get another parking ticket just so we could hook up again in the morning. Within a few weeks, it became difficult to reconcile the man I saw at the restaurant—collecting rounds of sangria at the service well or entering his orders into the POS system while generally avoiding my gaze— with the version I regularly encountered after my shift: sweating, biting his lower lip, gripping my naked flesh.

Maybe it was the secrecy with which Nic and I conducted our late-night sex romps that made it so exciting to me. It essentially repeated a habit I'd formed earlier in life. I'd learned growing up to hide my sexuality—to treat it as a kind of shameful secret.

Before I moved to Chicago, I lived in central Illinois for twenty years, most of that time spent in my parents' home, a welcoming white brick house with blue shutters. We took our Christmas photos out front in the fall maple foliage, my dad wearing plaid flannel and holding our family dog. A sidewalk wrapped from the front door around a tall evergreen tree, as if our house was throwing its arm around a good friend.

My parents, both from small towns, held fairly conservative family values. We went to church every Sunday until I decided to opt out. My father was a science-minded atheist who had recently stopped going as well. During my confirmation process, I'd asked our pastor how the seven-day theory of creation could be true given that it conflicted with the entire scientific field of paleontology. He sidestepped my concerns, telling me the seven days weren't meant to be read literally.

I realized I couldn't become a member of a church I didn't believe in. More concerning to me, though, was that if adults were willing to bullshit me about something as consequential as the afterlife, what else were they preaching that might not be true? The problem, I would soon learn, with using religion as a moral compass is you either stick to the prescribed path or become completely lost. There is no map for the gray area.

As I became a teenager in the late 90s, the gray areas inevitably presented themselves. When I was fourteen, at a high school football game, a nineteen-year-old basketball player asked if I wanted to meet him later that night. In the whole two months I'd been a freshman there, I'd seen Larson around school and knew he had knocked up a girl two years older than me. But I didn't care—*he had noticed me.*

At the time, I felt ugly. I had braces and wore boxy colorful sweaters. I thought sex was the key to unlocking the door to another world. If I could be seen as beautiful and desirable by men, popularity with women would surely follow. I agreed to meet him at 12:30 a.m. that night, which would require sneaking out.

I waited for my parents to fall asleep then crept out my front window, down the sidewalk, and past the evergreen tree where Larson was waiting in his car. He took me to a basement that smelled of stale cigarettes and beer. We left the lights off so as not to wake anyone. There, on top of a mattress on the floor, I lost my virginity.

I continued to see Larson like that for a few months. I became obsessed with him, even though he offered me nothing. He wasn't my boyfriend and didn't talk to me in the halls at school. But I wrote his name in my notebook, drew little hearts around it, even. I spent long rides on the bus to high school swim meets replaying our late-night rendezvous in my head.

I assumed we had to conduct our affair in private because of the age difference. But there was also the fact that everyone, including me, knew he had a baby momma at school—and she was due in the spring. A few months later, he stopped passing me notes in the halls and started avoiding me altogether.

At the end of the year, the girls in his graduating class put together a document they dubbed the Senior Will, traditionally used to "pass down" gifts—i.e., offensive descriptions of underclassmen—and distributed it around school. It said things like, "We leave Gabby Smith oyster crackers to go with her chili-smelling pussy." Everyone read it, including teachers, who confiscated copies.

In it, they called me a "whore" and left me an "STD kit," which was less original than Gabby Smith's inheritance—but harsher than what my best friend, Alex, was willed: "the full Buns-of-Steel collection on VHS." At the time, I didn't understand that contempt for women is actually something women can learn from each other.

I've always had feminist leanings but have spent much of my life without a community to fully support my emancipation—especially when it came to sex. Although my mother was a self-professed "women's libber," the sexual revolution had not rubbed off on her, at least not in a way she could share with her teenage daughter. The only people who found my sexuality appropriate—appealing even—were men.

So I offered myself to them in exchange for validation, which was often short-lived. For the most part, I accepted that sex would not necessarily lead to a relationship (though it sometimes did). It was almost better not to get attached—less risk of getting hurt. Operating like a man felt like liberation. But it required I suppress my feelings.

While at my museum internship in Chicago, I was supposed to enter data into a spreadsheet from an email sign-up list. Instead I found myself daydreaming about Nic ripping off my underwear so he could go down on me.

One morning after we'd been steadily seeing each other for a couple of months, I rode with him in a taxi. He was on his way to work, and I was on my way home—I hadn't driven the night before. I laid my head in his lap, and he caressed my hair with a subtle softness that would ultimately be my downfall. It was less intimate than, say, our mutual-masturbation race an hour before but more affectionate than our normal goodbyes, which involved a peck on the lips and a slap on the ass at best.

I knew this touch anywhere—it was that of a boyfriend. You don't caress someone you don't care about in such a way. But it was an isolated incident. He continued to keep me at arm's length, treating me as if I meant little to him. My mind received mixed signals. I found myself thinking about Nic more and more. It drove me crazy that he would only return my texts sometimes—and we only saw one another in the middle of the night. We'd begun our tryst in September, but it wasn't until February that he actually invited me somewhere during the day.

"Do you want to watch the Super Bowl with me later?" he asked the morning of the big game.

"Okay," I said apprehensively, worried he might have been just messing with my head.

I met him at a bar near his house that afternoon, even though I hate sports—especially football. I was just happy for the chance to be with him.

Fuck, I realized—I wanted to *be with* him.

True story: I hadn't been in this type of booty-call situation since I was seventeen, and my boyfriend Jack was serving six months in jail. I was a one-guy kind of gal—and for the most part, a loyal one, even as a prison wife. But six months was long enough to get bored, especially in a town where people partied at train tracks in the cornfields.

One night, I was hanging out at a party when I went to smoke weed in my car with a tall guy I had a crush on. (This has embarrassingly been my modus operandi for getting laid for a while.) I was about as smooth with my pickup lines as a fist through a piece of paper.

"Do you want to have sex?" I asked.

By this point, my desire for clandestine sexual encounters had already ingrained itself into my young psyche. Tall Guy's bed was low to the ground, a futon maybe, and when we had sex on it, he pulled my long blonde hair and called out my name in a throaty way none of my boyfriends ever had, "Sa-rahhhh."

Maybe it was the illicitness that added an extra air of excitement, or an unfamiliar voice with whom I shared no banal, everyday activities—no history of fighting over whether to rent *Le Divorce* or the latest *Terminator* movie at Blockbuster—that was inherently sexier. But again, what did I get from a man who could offer me nothing but secretive late-night sex on a mattress? I didn't know if it was degrading or empowering. Or if they were two sides of the same coin.

Not all of my sexual experiences have gone down like this. Later, my college boyfriend was committed and respectful and perfectly nice. But it didn't have that same "holy shit what are we doing" catastrophic element, which apparently I desired in a fuck buddy. When you really love someone, a best friend or a boyfriend, they become almost like a member of the family. You don't want to yell out dirty things to them, like *I'm going to cum on your face.*

"Nice" evoked a kind of caring that, up until a point, I only understood as fatherly. When I was a teenager, my father had given me a lecture about how sex was supposed to be an expression of love. I was so offended I covered my ears with my hands and rocked back and forth in my chair until it stopped.

I didn't fall for Tall Guy, but when Jack got out of the joint, he caught wind that something had gone down between us. His response: to physically assault me. Kindness, it turned out, was an important trait in a boyfriend. But for a booty call? I didn't think it really mattered. I assumed I could compartmentalize sex and love the way men did. Or that I should be able to, if we were truly equal.

The week before Valentine's Day, when I asked Nic what he would be doing that night, he told me, "Taking my girlfriend to dinner."

I braced myself on my kitchen sink.

"I thought you guys broke up," I said, my mind racing through a catalogue of what I'd assumed to be evidence that he'd been steadily becoming more available. There was, of course, the Super Bowl, where he'd put his arm around me in broad daylight, in front of friends. There were the women's hair care products in his bathroom, the contents of which had stayed at the same level since I'd been overnighting there. I used them once at his suggestion and wondered what kind of woman she'd *been*, past tense.

I'd mentally avoided the fact he only called me late at night and that a photograph of the two of them remained on the windowsill. She had pale blonde hair and a pretty smile. The guys at work said she looked like Anna Kournikova, the tennis player and subject of Enrique Iglesias's creepy hit song about running and hiding but not being able to escape his love. Once, Nic asked me if an earring he'd found by his bedside was mine. It wasn't.

We'd been seeing each other on and off for four months, but to be fair, there was never any assumption of exclusivity or coupledom. A man who wants to date you takes your ass out to dinner. I'd originally assumed I would be satisfied with an intermittent, no-strings-attached arrangement, but over the course of a few months, my feelings changed. Nic had been to my house, in my bed, where he experienced the most intimate side of me.

He'd even called me at midnight on my birthday a month before. Why would he do that?

I felt not cheated on but still cheated somehow.

"You don't understand," he told me. "She's sick."

I had no idea how to even begin to process this information. My roommate was not impressed.

"That guy is a dick," she said.

I eventually got a job at a different restaurant, where I projected my desires on another male bartender out of sheer convenience, but he didn't seem even a little bit interested. I met an attractive six-foot-three lawyer with an MBA who I really tried to like. But he was (cringe) nice. So instead, I found myself hopelessly thinking about Nic, who offered no perks besides feeding my fixation on him.

In the next few months, it became clear to me my lust for Nic's attention was no longer sustainable. This revelation occurred during a pre-Tinder era, when meeting men, stigma-free anyway, was limited to IRL. I heard stories of him hitting on other women—friends of friends—and decided his girlfriend couldn't be that sick, and if she was, then he was *really* an asshole, as opposed to just your run-of-the-mill rake.

A month or so would go by between our meetups. Eventually, he stopped returning my texts, and I stopped sending them. Still, some part of me was holding onto the belief that if I were truly special, he would come to realize it. And that was precisely the problem—my specialness was riding on whether or not some guy liked me. As early as fourteen, I'd begun valuing and devaluing myself based on approval from men.

This was all, of course, before empowerment went mainstream, trended on social media, and became a commodity to be packaged and sold to women by corporations. In the late '90s and the early '00s, there was no Jezebel or #YesAllWomen or widespread anti-slut-shaming movements. Fucking whomever you wanted, whenever you wanted, felt like a solitary act of feminism, regardless of the fallout.

For me, like many other women, the #MeToo movement came too late.

The winter I spent sleeping with Nic, I was also raped. I had texted Nic earlier that night to see if he was around and received what had become a familiar response: silence. By this time, I knew he didn't care, and I hated myself for wanting him to. So I went to another guy's house, willingly, not thinking anything out of the ordinary would happen.

I saw Nic again afterward but never told him about it. One night several months later, in a traumatized state of denial and drunken stupor, I called, cursed him out, and then hung up. Some part of me blamed him for not being there to protect me. But it was drowned out by a larger part of me that blamed myself.

To admit you need protection is to confess vulnerability. It's not something I would have done at the time. I did not yet understand that true intimacy requires a different kind of nakedness than the one I excelled in. Nor did I know that I would not be satisfied stripping off my clothes, all while keeping my emotions guarded.

Not long ago, I got an email from LinkedIn that said, "People are looking at your profile." "People" turned out to be Nic. I was thirty-three and had only recently started going to therapy for the rape. I hadn't spoken to Nic in ten years but had coincidentally been rolling the thought of us around in my mind. I saw him not only as a man from my past who had hurt me but also a portal to a less wounded self.

Since I didn't know how else to reach Nic, in order to send him a message, I had to first invite him to connect with me on LinkedIn. What better way to examine a dark part of your past than the unforgiving fluorescent light of a professional networking site?

Because my drunken call had been our last contact, I opened with some brief greetings and an apology: *I would like to apologize to you for the way I left things—not a good time in my life. Call it making amends if you want, I just felt the need to tell you that.* I secretly hoped he would think I was in AA and not pining for him.

I don't know why you're apologizing, he responded. *I was the one who was a complete jackass.*

Yes, you were, I wrote back, relieved.

We exchanged a few more cordial messages, and it was clear he didn't think I was dumb or slutty or desperate. Is that what *I* had thought this whole time? I realized my unresolved feelings had more to do with me than they did him. Like the men who had come before, he was a mirror I'd held up in hopes of seeing myself in a more flattering light. And I'd given far too much authority to what I saw in the reflection.

A few years have since passed, and though I haven't spoken to Nic, I often wonder what would happen if we saw each other again. Would our fling feel like ancient history? Or would I start drooling like one of Pavlov's dogs? When I was twenty, I ran into the basketball player from my high school at a nightclub, who would have been twenty-five by then. I could see him staring at me from across the room, his jaw dropped wide open. He didn't even attempt to close it as I walked past. To his credit, I probably looked a lot different without braces.

APOLLO'S REVELATION

Look I am not in any way capable of rape! I cannot see how you cannot realize that when that happened and you told me to stop and I did.

The man who emailed me this confounding set of phrases was responding to a message I'd sent him about an incident that had happened ten years before. When I went looking for his email address in 2015, I found an article from 2005 that said he'd been hit in the head with a crowbar, which maybe explained a lot.

There is no easy way to say this, I wrote in the email. *You raped me.*

I hadn't challenged him at the time because I'd been in shock—confused by the idea that someone I knew could have raped me. In the U.S., the federal definition of rape hadn't yet changed to center around the lack of consent as opposed to the use of force. And though the meaning of the word has shifted throughout history, it's always carried a seed of the same idea, from the Latin root *rapere*: to seize or take by force, haste, or fury; to ravish; to snatch. That's what he'd done. He'd pounced. He'd hastily taken advantage. He'd snatched.

I want you to think about what you are saying before the word rape is used. I moved faster than you were comfortable with. For that I am truly sorry. When you said stop I did. I can't take back that moment.

I didn't fully grasp the meaning of rape until I viewed a 17th-century baroque portrayal at the Villa Borghese museum in Rome. Gian Lorenzo Bernini's sculpture *The Rape of Proserpina* does not depict a "rape" in the contemporary sense of the word but as it was used then—an abduction with the intent to forcibly marry, which carries many of the same hallmarks, the most obvious being implied sexual servitude.

In the Roman myth, Proserpina, daughter of Ceres, was picking flowers in Sicily when Pluto emerged from Mt. Etna with four black horses and dragged her back down to the underworld. Her mother, the goddess of grains and agriculture, caused a famine in retaliation and negotiated a deal with Pluto to allow Proserpina to return to the world of the living for six months out of every year. The myth became an origin story for spring and Proserpina a symbol for reemergence.

What is most striking in Bernini's rendering is how it evokes both sensuality and horror, as Pluto's muscular body overtakes Proserpina's feminine curves—his large hands digging into her soft flesh, which, for a moment, one forgets is made from Carrera marble. Her body contorts in an attempt to turn away from what her face tells us she already knows will be her fate. Fabric hangs loosely from their half-naked bodies as Cerberus, the three-headed dog, stands guard below foreshadowing what will become her lifelong ties to the underworld.

Ok I need to know that you understand that if you tell someone to stop and they do that it's not rape. Yes I jumped the gun and yes I crossed the line and did so without asking most likely after misunderstanding a cue that you prolly never meant to give.

Just a few rooms away in the Villa Borghese, in another Bernini sculpture, *Apollo and Daphne*, a magnificent scene unfolds: A nymph is transforming into a laurel tree to avoid the romantic advances of a god. In the Roman myth, Eros (better known by the Greeks as Cupid), has shot Apollo with a golden arrow and Daphne with lead. Apollo cannot break the spell of his desire for Daphne who is in turn repulsed by him. He chases her, and she flees, finally asking her father, a river god, to help her escape.

The sculpture demonstrates how quickly desire can slip into violence: the moment of Daphne's transformation—and of Apollo's revelation, as he catches up with her and realizes something has gone terribly wrong. Leaves have sprouted from her fingertips and roots from her feet. His hand reaches for her stomach to find only bark, but he is not dissuaded.

As the story is originally described in Ovid's *Metamorphoses*, "Embracing the branches as though they were still limbs he kissed the wood, but even as wood, she shrank from his kisses." Apollo decided she would still be his as a tree, and the leaves on her branches, rustling in the wind, seemed to nod in consent. Ovid thus places the burden on the reader to decide whether Daphne, now a laurel tree, actually offered her consent. For centuries, rape has been considered a mutable concept, its existence dependent on the eye of the beholder.

I must have thought you were into it and made a very forward move without asking, which is not ok! But if you had in any way told me to stop before that happened it simply would never have taken place.

A story so old it's written in stone.

We were kissing, and I wasn't into it. So I lay curled up in a protective pose on top of his bed to take a quick nap. It seemed like the easiest way to simultaneously get out of rejecting someone I would have to see at work and to sober up before driving home. My body felt heavy as lead, impenetrable as rock—as uninviting as a tree.

For a moment, I was in a dream.

A hand was slowly unzipping my pants, and whatever it was doing down there sent warm sensations tingling through my body. As I awoke, his head found its way between my legs. I didn't want it there, but I also didn't fight the feeling. My branches bent and my body shuddered with unwelcome pleasure. His hands reached for the flesh of my thighs, gripped them, and dragged my hips down to the end of his bed.

Before I could react, he had forced himself on me.

"Stop," I said twice, my body moving up and down, before his eyes met mine and something in his brain seemed to click.

Apollo's revelation.

He rolled off me. We were both still wearing our shirts. I turned away so my back was facing him, and he slung his arm over my shoulder.

I hope you realize that I am not angry but just confused as to why with so much horrible sexual assault out there that you would attribute this to something like rape.

A small study, "Denying Rape but Endorsing Forceful Intercourse," surveyed seventy-two college-age men. One in three admitted they would be willing to use force or coercion to obtain sex—as long as there would not be consequences. But when researchers replaced descriptions of forced or coerced sex with the word "rape," the number dropped to one in ten. The research showed that this smaller group of respondents held more overtly hostile attitudes toward women—whereas the remainder, the twenty percent that would rape as long as you didn't call it rape, were simply callous, perceiving a women's "no" as nothing more than token resistance.

Pluto takes pride in his actions. Apollo hides behind Cupid's bow.

Which is the greater threat?

I AM SORRY, for moving too fast for you that night. I AM SORRY that it got as far as it did. But most of all I am SORRY you think it is ok to accuse someone of something like this TEN YEARS LATER!

I didn't fully appreciate *The Rape of Proserpina* until I saw it again, nearly a decade after my own rape—the sensual thrill I'd first experienced as a viewer now inextricably linked with the terror in her eyes. Bernini had carefully carved out Proserpina's irises to create a shadow that would outline her pupils. His portraiture is known for its intimacy, and the malleability he creates can be credited to a style he pioneered known as the "speaking likeness" that is capturing an expression just before or after an utterance.

He once explained, "To make a successful portrait, one should choose an action and attempt to represent it well; that the best time to render the mouth is when [the subject] has just spoken or is just about to begin speaking; that one should try to catch this moment." Based on the way Proserpina's head is tilted to one side as she pulls away from Pluto, two teardrops running down her cheek, her lips and teeth parted slightly, it appears she is about to say something. Perhaps it was going to be "no."

VIRTUES OF PLOP

We were supposed to be taking a group quiz in accounting lab, and the way Erik tells it, I was "being a gigantic nerd." His bright-blue eyes darted back and forth as he snuck our textbook open on his lap. "You're going to get us in trouble," I said through clenched teeth. But our professor didn't seem to notice.

Erik was broad-shouldered with pale skin, short wisps of blonde hair, and a long, straight nose—features that cumulatively reminded me of a polar bear. We were both sophomores at the University of Illinois, and once we became friends, I realized he was the only person I'd ever met with a taste for lowbrow culture relative to such a high-powered intellect. We'd sit together watching stoner flicks, like *Jay and Silent Bob Strike Back*, in between solving derivatives for our macroeconomics class.

I liked being with him and didn't find there was any sexual tension between us. I'd never had a brother, or any other kind of relationship with a man where there was no pressure to be anything other than myself.

Around the same time I met Erik, I started dating a tall, good-looking, clean-shaven guy named Mike with dark hair who resembled Bobby from *Twin Peaks*. A fifth-year senior and finance major from a wealthy suburb, he lived in one of the most expensive buildings on campus. When we were together, I found myself imitating his cockiness, usually to hide my own insecurities that I wasn't pretty or sophisticated enough. Mike often commented on women's appearances, remarking on their relative "hotness," which made me feel I had to labor to keep up. I wore tight clothing and excessive makeup. Once, I teetered in wooden stilettos on my old stained carpeting, wearing a denim miniskirt and an off-the-shoulder blouse.

"We're just going to dinner," he said.

I was overacting for a role I'd never before been cast: trophy girlfriend. At the time, I found the idea that I could be seen as beautiful or valuable by someone like him to be thrilling. But in hindsight, I much preferred hanging out with Erik.

Aristotle believed that *philia*, or friendship—one of the many types of love identified by the ancient Greeks—required familiarity, virtue, and equality. This is not the same as what we call "platonic love" today, a concept originally rooted in Plato's idea that through eros, or erotic love, one can transcend the physical and access the divine.

In *Symposium,* Plato theorizes that we desire what has been mysteriously omitted from us by a divine force, and thus to become more ourselves, we seek it out in someone else. Following Platonic logic, my relationship with Mike was doomed; he did not possess that which was lacking from my true self. I was still in the process of carving out my identity, and he made me feel less—not more—who I was.

Being with Erik, on the other hand, was like looking into a rare mirror that revealed both the attractive and unattractive parts and somehow still left me feeling good about them. After Mike graduated college and moved away, we stayed in a long-distance relationship, but I got to spend the summer with Erik on an empty campus. We ate gigantic burritos at our favorite Mexican restaurant, then held our bulging stomachs groaning about how sick we felt. On the weekends, we drove to my grandparents' lake house in southern Illinois, blaring our favorite Outkast album, *Aquemini*, as the flat prairie land morphed into rolling hills. Erik fished from a dock while I sunbathed on a raft. We paddled my grandpa's Budweiser-branded canoe out to explore nearby coves using long wooden oars. Every once in a while, I'd hear, "dammit, Kasbeer" because I'd somehow managed to get water on our stash or soak our cigarettes without actually paddling us anywhere.

When we returned to shore, we'd sit on the edge of the seawall and play a game we invented called the Plop Game. It involved taking turns dropping rocks into the water and laughing when they made a "plop" sound. Each round, the more impressive "plop" garnered a point. I'm pretty sure when Plato defined the type of love that transcends the physical as a "pregnancy of the soul," the Plop Game was not what he had in mind. He proposed a spiritual love that went beyond self-fulfillment, attainable only through the recognition of what is good, what is beautiful, and what is true.

In Rachel Cusk's novel *Outline*, she writes of a similar ideal, a shared vision: "It is one definition of love, the belief in something that only the two of you can see." Erik and I were nearly always in agreement on whose "plop" had won the round.

The summer after my junior year, Erik hurt his foot playing softball, and since no one was around to help him, he stayed with me. At the time, my apartment had a few roaches that mainly came out at night. There was also a squirrel biting through one of the plastic accordion arms of my window air conditioner. After a weekend spent with Mike in Chicago, I came home to find two beady little black eyes staring at me through a squirrel-sized hole.

"If only we could pit the squirrels against the roaches," Erik said.

I put a cutting board over the hole, but the squirrel scratched at it every night. Since Erik couldn't walk for a few days, he stayed at my place with his foot elevated. Having him there made me feel safer, given my double infestation. He refused to go to the doctor, despite the fact that his lower leg had turned purple and taken on the shape of a ski boot. I got us carry-out dinners and rented him the Civil War epic *Gettysburg*.

Because I was afraid of the roaches, I slept next to him and his undiagnosed leg fracture. I found my large, bearded slumber-buddy to be comforting. He was like a brother to me and never stared at me creepily or anything. But it further muddied the definition of our relationship. I didn't understand what I could have with a man if it didn't involve romance or sex.

My senior year in college, I studied abroad in Italy, and Erik and I met in Amsterdam to indulge in our favorite activities. We played endless games of checkers at coffee shops, visited the van Gogh museum, and took pictures of ourselves with life-size wax figures of Arnold Schwarzenegger and Bill Clinton. At a casino, I won fifty Euros on the slot machine. There's a photo of us sitting at the bar afterward, and when I saw it later, I noticed my own toothy grin in contrast with his downward gaze and the protective way his oversized hand gripped my shoulder.

After college, I lived in Chicago and remained in an on-again, off-again with Mike, depending on how bored I was with my alternative prospects. One night, Erik and I had gone out to a dive bar down the street from my apartment ("the one with the Schlitz sign in the window," we called it). He was staying at my place to avoid having to drive back to the West Side where his mom lived. When we got back, buzzed, I set him up on an Ikea couch, which was about as comfortable as folded cardboard. He grimaced.

"Can't I just sleep in the bed?"

I hesitated, remembering the Amsterdam photo.

"C'mon, dude," he said. "Please."

How do you set boundaries for a relationship you can't even define?

"Are you in love with me?" I asked.

He looked offended.

"No, Sarah."

He rolled onto his other side to face the back of the sofa. I walked back into my bedroom, cringing. What was I hoping he would say? "Yes," so I would have had to tell him I didn't feel the same, at least not in a romantic sense, thereby ruining whatever kind of relationship it was that we had? When I woke up the next morning, he was already gone.

Plato believed love to be selfish: The lover desires something specific from the beloved, and therefore the love is inherently conditional. But the condition is simply that the person become more himself. In this view, love is a kind of recognition, writes philosophy scholar Aryeh Kosman in *Virtues of Thought.* "It is seeing another as what that other might be, not in the sense of what he might be other than himself, but how he might be what he is. It is, in other words, coming to recognize the *beauty* of another."

Mutual self-actualization, in this theory, is merely a pleasant side effect of dual selfishness. But just because you see the beauty in someone doesn't make them the right person to self-actualize with. The summer after we graduated college, Erik moved to Poland for an internship—and ended up staying there. Before he left, he gave me a copy of his favorite book, *Things Fall Apart.* Afterward, I sat in my car crying.

It's not so easy to replace your platonic soul mate. Although I did try. Years later, I married a man I'd been good friends with first. But after the relationship became romantic, our egos began to obscure what was good, what was beautiful, and what was true. In order to see your real self reflected back, you have to be willing to show the other person who you are.

Plato's inquiry into love revealed it to be an inquiry into the self—an endless discovery in which a final form is never rendered. In the fifteen years that Erik has lived across the Atlantic, we've stayed in touch. When we do get together, we tend to conform to our original roles, which hold a kernel of truth about who we are still—he the bold eccentric and I the gigantic nerd. The yin to his yang. Two mutually exclusive shapes that collectively form some kind of whole, whatever you want to call it.

Laurenz was the kind of man who owned bearskin rugs—with the heads still attached. I looked one of them squarely in the eye as I waited in his Manhattan apartment for a $5,000 sofa to be delivered from Italy. After it arrived, I checked his floorboards to ensure the deliverymen hadn't left any footprints or scratches, packed up the cardboard, winced at the flattened bear carcasses, and then, like a good assistant, took his recycling out to the curb.

He was the creative director for several European fashion magazines, based remotely out of a boutique design studio in New York City. In exchange for his name on the publications' mastheads, he chose the cover models, what they wore, and how they would be photographed—usually sprawled out somewhere on a black sand beach in the Canary Islands.

As his assistant, I influenced whether his guests would receive their coffee in a timely manner, where his driver would pick him up, and what kind of toilet paper to buy for the office. As part of my duties, I had to be ready at any moment for him to call me with an urgent request for a helicopter to pick up a client on set in Montauk—or for directions to a restaurant in Geneva and to "pronounce it like it should sound in French."

An awkward Midwestern transplant in my mid-twenties, I was hoping the job would be my entrée into the behind-the-scenes world of magazine production. The Craigslist ad I answered had stipulated: "Design Studio with Luxury Advertising and Editorial Clients Seeking Assistant to Busy Creative

Director." In a screening interview with the business manager, an example task she presented me with was ensuring that Mr. Dolce and Mr. Gabbana in Milan receive their flower arrangements in a timely manner—and that the flowers reflect the proper aesthetic of the studio. Apparently, the last assistant had failed at this task.

"Laurenz is a brilliant creative director," she said. "But very particular."

Alarm bells were going off in the back of my head, but I tuned them out and chose instead to think about how I'd be on a first-name basis with the florist and the clients in no time. I imagined myself twirling around in a leather office chair while making important phone calls.

"*Vittorio, I need something striking for Miuccia!*"

My ballooning dream world was punctured by another red flag when I found out that the person I would deal with in my day-to-day was only willing to give up five minutes to meet with me before offering me the job. But I shoved my inklings down into the pit of my stomach—near where I kept worries about credit card debt and the need for catastrophic health insurance.

A distinguished blonde man in his forties, Laurenz had the sort of old-world charm that came with vintage timepieces, expertly tailored wool suits, and a thick Austrian accent. He was definitely the most tastefully styled heterosexual man I'd ever encountered. Though I knew he was married, I found the way he looked right through the women in his office, including me, to be both comforting and a little disturbing.

Maybe it was his job; staring at photos of supermodels all day had rendered him immune to women who were anything less than dazzling in appearance. Other evidence suggested he might be a psychopath. What he lacked in empathy, he made up for in eccentricity, a trait that is often confused with "creative genius," creating a permission structure for its owner to remain completely untethered to reality. In the three years I worked for him, I saw him eating only once, when he walked into the office on a summer day wearing overalls with ticking stripes, wide-eyed and clutching a red Popsicle.

Laurenz was a busy man who split his time between New York and Europe. Often, our encounters occurred via raging emails about his travel arrangements. He would ask me to make calls on his behalf requesting special last-minute accommodations. Let's say he wanted a free upgraded seat on his flight in row one or two of first class, and by the way, he's running late so you'll have to hold the plane.

"Sorry," his travel agent once told me. "I tried that once for Kate Moss."

I found that the biggest problem with asking for favors for Laurenz was that, as far as I could tell, no one seemed to know or care who he was—a fact that never quite seemed to sink in for him. I didn't mind the creative challenge of talking him up so much as the discomfort of slowly backing away from his desk after delivering the news that my attempts had failed.

Such efforts included begging for him without shame, especially when it came to tasks like nabbing him a seat at the Celine show during Paris fashion week. Effectively managing Laurenz's fashion show agenda should have resulted in multiple restraining orders against me. Each season, I became an intercontinental stalker, systematically emailing, calling, and texting all of the publicists in America and Europe until I received an answer about whether they could give him a seat at their show, and cringe—please not farther back than the third row.

We could never speak of the time he was seated next to Sasha Baron Cohen, who was masquerading as "Brüno from Austrian Gay TV" for his 2009 movie.

If the answer was no, Laurenz would pull out the magical cell phone number of the person in charge, and when I finally got that person on the phone, he or she would let out an exasperated sigh followed by, "I'll see what I can do." Once, I learned even Kanye had been turned away at the door to a show I'd gotten Laurenz into, and I finally understood the true meaning of the word *schadenfreude*.

Of course, it didn't always work out this way, since fashion people have different ideas of who is important. The industry selects its image-makers carefully—or fickly, depending on who you ask. "I do not invite the Art Director of American *Vogue*," one French publicist told me through her caramel accent, "Why on earth would I invite your boss?" *Look, lady, I just want to go home and watch* The Wire *on Netflix, so the sooner we stop talking about this, the sooner I can be reprimanded and call you back.*

When performing menial tasks over and over, I've found it's best to make up some kind of fake challenge to pass the time. I learned this at my first job at fifteen back in Illinois. I wasn't legally old enough to work for minimum wage, so I made something like $4.75 an hour after school working as the fry girl at McDonald's in a red visor and pleated polyester pants. I have not forgotten how the pants sounded, the swooshing of polyester as I cut strategically through the back alleys on my way to work.

To pass the time, I made a game out of the fry grill, scooping the fries into their red greasy buckets and lining them up: five in the back row, four in the middle, three in the next. I created a pyramid that I would challenge myself to keep full, no matter how fast the salty sticks flew off my triangular production line.

I'm certain that my formative years as a fry girl contributed to my later-in-life affinity for the luxury business: I secretly hoped that an embossed leather Prada bag would un-emboss the golden arches from my soul.

It turned out that the mental coping skills I'd acquired while working at McDonald's paid off in my professional endeavors. While straightening up Laurenz's library a decade later, I invented a similar game: I'd guess how many vintage issues of *Harper's Bazaar* Paris would fit on one shelf and then line them up to test my theory. Sometimes I'd mix it up and stagger book spines by color or stack them in order of height.

Once, while standing on a stepladder, I noticed two giant black garbage bags behind a stack of dusty, '70s photography books. As part of my office-organizing duties, I was supposed to label everything using a system; e.g., BOOK_VINTAGE NUDES.

I pulled one of the garbage bags toward me as a layer of dust cascaded downward. When I opened it, I felt what one never wants to feel when voluntarily sticking one's hand into a dark container: furry things. The bag was filled with foxtails—with partial skins still attached. I could tell by the soft, bouncy feel of the second that it contained the same. There must have been at least fifty of them. I nearly toppled over the ladder and had to collect myself before proceeding with the label maker. I began to type C-A-D-A-V-E-R-S_F-O-X.

"You have to apologize," said Natasha, a six-foot German project manager with dark hair and olive skin who bossed me around while Laurenz was away—and sometimes when he was there. He spoke English but occasionally would prefer to bark orders in German, and then have her translate them to me. Like most of the studio's designers from across the pond, she was there on an H-1 or "special ability" visa, which if indeed was legitimate, I speculated must have had something to do with angry-typing. People in administrative jobs rarely have irreplaceable skill sets.

"What am I apologizing for again?"

I already knew the answer. Laurenz had been on the way back from a photo shoot in Morocco, and apparently the airline had made a mistake and not listed his name on the flight manifest. The was particularly strange because I'd gone out of my way to confirm his ticket with the travel agent and sat on hold with Royal Air Maroc for an hour just to ensure he got an aisle seat.

"The inconvenience that this caused him," Natasha continued.

I envisioned poor Laurenz in the first class line, twirling his blonde beard and then beating his angry fists on the counter.

"So that he won't think you're incompetent," the studio's business manager whispered to me. I began to type:

> *Dear Laurenz,*
>
> *I'm terribly sorry for the inconvenience. I double confirmed with the travel agent and airline, but they must have made a mistake and will refund the money you paid at check-in. I will do everything in my power so that this doesn't happen again.*
>
> *Apologies,*
>
> *Sarah*

When I hit send, I could feel a piece of my soul traveling with it—in coach.

The worst thing about making thirty thousand dollars a year in New York City as an assistant at a small company is watching the boss use his company credit card like a personal ATM. Five hundred dollars at Il Buco. Seven hundred at Yves Saint Laurent. Two hundred and fifteen euros in the *Flughafen* (airport) shops in Vienna. At some point, I decided to even the score.

It started small—I would order multiple tins of coffee from illy and take one of them home. He owes me, I'd think while sipping my over-roasted yet reassuringly Italian espresso. A box of tampons there, a bag of dishwasher packs here—what was the harm? No one would ever notice that I was skimming off the office supplies because I was the only person who kept track of them. I started carrying an extra bag when I went to the Duane Reade.

I worked every night until eight, sometimes just to wait for a designer to finish layouts so I could hand-carry the printouts to FedEx. It wasn't the long hours or low pay that really bothered me—although, if you had asked me at the time, I would have said, "the long hours and the low pay." Not to mention the myriad of personal tasks that cropped up at all hours of the night, from the banal to the bizarre, like calling every resort in Tulum because Laurenz's wife wasn't happy with the one he chose—or overnighting a book from Amazon titled *How to Teach Your Baby to Be Physically Superb*.

But by far the most humiliating charge was when he made me send an email to the entire office explaining the *raison d'être* of a toilet brush. I may have been lucky to have a job, but I paid for it in sleepless nights, depleted self-esteem, and the constant anxiety of being tethered to my boss through an iPhone.

He owes me, I thought as I absconded with an external hard drive. I knew he padded his bill with clients, so I figured, why shouldn't I pad mine with him? Bad behavior, it turns out, can easily become contagious.

"Do you have to do that so loudly?" Natasha scowled as I packaged up some photographic proofs to be sent to a magazine in London. This was strange because she was the one who demanded I laminate packages with shipping tape in case it happened to be raining at the other end of the FedEx route. Next, I'd been instructed by her to clean out some of our filing drawers. We kept one filled with samples of different print techniques—luscious, gilded paper stocks, expensive invitations, and high-end catalogues.

"Throw them out, we don't have room," she ordered.

As I carried a stack to its final resting place, I noticed one book in particular. It had dark, moody photographs and was printed on a heavy version of tissue paper. I decided to rescue it from the recycling bin. I'd made a habit of collecting useless ephemera. Under my bed were boxes filled with fancy collaging papers, photographs, and books. Like any borderline hoarder will tell you, it's not what they're for but what they *could* be for that matters. When I got home later that night and examined the book more carefully, I realized it was an artist's proof of a limited edition series valued at around $3,000.

For almost three years, I hunkered down at my desk, shoulders pulled up to my ears, bracing for a verbal attack, which under the watchful eye of Natasha and Laurenz could come at any moment from any direction. One stormy afternoon, I picked up a particularly frightening call from Laurenz. He didn't say hello, but it was pretty obvious who it was.

"VERE IST MY CAR!"

"It should be there. I'll call the service and call you back." I told him. He was at home getting ready to leave for the airport, and I'd booked him a car as usual, but apparently there were weather delays and the service had failed to notify me.

"Ten minutes," the dispatcher told me.

I'd done the job long enough to know that in New York City car-service speak, "ten minutes" meant "not soon." I immediately called two other companies, but since he was already leaving on a rainy Friday at 4:30 p.m. in lower Manhattan, there were no drivers to be found. When this had happened in the past, I was forced to go downstairs, run to his house nearby, and try to hail him a taxi. But in this case, there was really no time. While I was still on hold, Laurenz beeped in on the other line.

"VERE IST MY CAR?"

I tried to explain that he'd likely have to go outside and look for one, but my words were drowned out by him screaming the same question over and over, louder and louder. I began to wonder how I'd let things get to this point. It was a vicious cycle: the longer I put up with his abuses, the more they cumulatively weighed on my self-esteem. The lower my self-esteem, the more likely I was to continue accepting my role as a poorly compensated doormat.

At that point, I did something I'd never done before: I hung up. I'd like to say it was an act of defiance—my way of finally standing up to his bullying. But really, it was just an involuntary reaction to the screaming. Instead of listening to it like I always did, I chucked the phone back at the receiver and resolved to let the cards fall where they may.

Alas, Laurenz did not fire me for this transgression, and my longstanding dream of sustaining on extended unemployment did not come true. The entire time I worked in his studio, I was looking for another job, and unsuccessfully so. Blame the financial crisis of 2008, my Midwestern truth-telling tendencies, or just bad karma from the "borrowing" of office supplies—but it took almost three years to find work elsewhere.

The main problem with a career in the fashion industry is that it only really qualifies you to work deeper in the fashion industry and simultaneously disqualifies you from everything else. Once you've proven you can hack it for a few years, fashion people accept you as one of their own and bring you further into the fold, whereas people in other industries increasingly view your skills as niche. A proven ability to possess Giselle Bündchen's private cell number and restrain yourself from drunk-texting her isn't exactly cover letter material.

At some point, I thought I wanted to become an art director. I took graphic design classes on the side—mainly for fun, but also to retouch my occasional butt-chin out of family photos. But one night, after staying late to edit a proposal for a project, it occurred to me that I might make an even better copywriter. Anyone who can sell an office on using a toilet brush via email is destined to go far.

One of the last calls I made on behalf of Laurenz was to American Airlines. He was taking a personal vacation to go skiing in Whistler, and I had held him a flight to Vancouver while I accumulated an exhaustive list of all airlines and flight times, which he preferred to scan in a matter of seconds before approving any purchase. When he was satisfied and I called to book the ticket, the agent told me there was no flight held in his name and the airfare had gone up considerably.

Before I could stop myself, a string of expletives followed by the word "idiot" flew past my lips.

"What did you just call me?" the agent asked.

Her Southern drawl reminded me more of where I came from than where I'd ended up.

"Nothing," I quickly corrected myself. "Nothing, I'm sorry."

She hesitated, and I could hear the tension crackling as she considered whether to hang up on me. I felt my face turn red and secretly wished she could see it. I apologized again. Slowly, she walked me through the other options, which I would have to take back to a very pissed off boss. By then, I was mostly upset that I'd somehow managed to completely lose myself in the shuffle.

When I finally found a job at another creative agency in a role that didn't involve being the liaison to a travel agent, I told Laurenz I was leaving.

"Are you sure?" he said. "I am happy with your performance." If my mouth hadn't been clenched shut in fear, my lower jaw would have landed squarely on his bespoke drafting table. Why would he have constantly whisper-screamed at someone who was doing a good job? By the time I'd survived the hazing and been let into the club, I no longer wanted to join.

I had a brief moment when I looked around at the gallery-white walls, vintage art books, and artfully worn leather furniture and thought about staying. Then I realized that A) I might have Stockholm syndrome, and B) I couldn't live in New York City for much longer on my salary.

I kept the $3,000 book for several years. It hid under my bed but never quite left the back of my mind. I entertained the idea of selling it but decided that since it didn't belong to me, I had no choice but to mail it back to its rightful owner. I did this via an unmarked box without any note or explanation. What would I say? One of your henchmen was going to throw it away so I kind-of-sort-of accidentally stole this and then had a change of heart?

I knew from experience that Laurenz got a lot of strange objects in the mail that no one questioned—the weirdest being a piece of a dead snake in an unmarked box. The dried-out rattle had sat on my desk for months until he finally claimed it, looking annoyed as if I'd purposely withheld it from him.

I looked at the book one more time before sealing it the box with an excessive amount of clear shipping tape. I then took it to the post office and dropped it into a bin at one of the self-serve mailing stations with no return address. The resulting thud was one I'd heard many times before, on evenings spent escorting packages to FedEx. But this one sounded by far the best.

SACRED STORIES

When I was a little girl, my favorite room in our house was my father's study. Furnished with a wall of scientific books, an old Macintosh, and a leather recliner, it had an air of intellectualism that I tried to absorb through osmosis. In the evenings, my dad and I played a mix of chess and Carmen Sandiego on our family computer, which in the 90s had so many pieces it required its own multi-compartment cabinet. On the weekends, I'd peer in through the cracked door to find him reading *National Geographic* or David McCullough. One wall held a giant topographic map of the world in striated shades of aqua and beige. My eyes lingered over the places I found most mysterious: the horn of Africa, the southern tip of South America, and the dark blue depths of the Mariana Trench.

My father was the arbiter of knowledge in our house, especially of the geopolitical variety. In fifth grade, he prepped me so well for the geography bee that I won the county—a media coup in Central Illinois. A photo of me smiling and holding a globe ran in the local newspaper. I even got to go on the radio. In science classes, I racked up piles of extra credit by memorizing and labeling each individual part of the human anatomical system, which I gleaned from my father's medical books. By high school, my dad was completing my physics projects for me at a college level.

But as I aged, I began to turn away from our nerdy little den and into my own foul-mouthed, cigarette-smoking, law-breaking mess of teenage delinquency. My father became not Dad the Great, but "Da-ad" the Ultimate Embarrassment. Dad the Lecturer. Dad who had no right to tell me what to do. The once constantly ticking mind of a curious child had transformed into an anxiety-ridden thought factory that required palliative deadening. I started smoking pot regularly but still managed to get good grades—with Dad's help. When we stopped getting along altogether, he hired an outside tutor.

By seventeen, I began to struggle emotionally, and my father completed my college applications for me. He applied only to programs that didn't require an essay—and his safety schools became my salvation. Back then I planned not to go to college. I was spending more and more time with Jack, who was dealing weed. My parents disliked him based on the fact that he had a criminal record, but they weren't aware of the level to which they should have been concerned. Neither was I. But then again, my father was the only man I really knew.

Jack was the size of a linebacker and a year and a half older than me. As a juvenile he'd already amassed a history of violent charges for fighting with other guys and putting his fist through a window. Since I'd always been on his good side, I never thought much about it. Once at school, I complained to him about how my childhood friend's older brother, who had terrorized me since I was little, had given me a hard time during gym class. The next day, he approached me in the hall and apologized, which I later learned had been Jack's doing.

"I made him get down on his knees," he told me after school.

Jack's dad owned an appliance business, but he lived with his mom, who had no job that I knew of. He wore the kind of boxy T-shirts and fraying jeans of someone life hadn't handed much in the way of privilege. I couldn't picture my friend's brother, having only recently transferred from a private school, clad in chinos and expensive sweaters, down on his knees, his face nearing Jack's size thirteen Timberlands. Half of me was terrified, and the other half thrilled. I felt flattered, protected—taken care of, even.

I spent all of my time at Jack's house, although I usually refused to disclose my whereabouts to my parents. That is, until he finally exploded on me. I don't remember much from that time period, as any memory not clouded by PTSD evaporated into a bong hit.

I do, however, recall having an argument with my dad in my bedroom that I assume had something to do with Jack. I'm not sure what about— only that my father sat on my bed and cried. His shoulders shook, a wave of emotion rose, and then tears came out of his eyes. At the time, I didn't know what to do with such a display of caring. I didn't think I deserved compassion, nor did I know how to receive it. It was much easier to turn away from him and continue down the path I thought I'd chosen for myself.

I was a freshman at the University of Illinois when George W. Bush was first elected president. I hadn't voted. If anyone asked, I would say it wasn't a popular election, and I lived in a blue state. The truth is I was lazy and stoned, and my method of transportation had been recently stolen when I attached my

U-lock to the metal rack but forgot to also secure the bike.

For someone surrounded by corn and soybean fields, the events of September 11, 2001, were surreal. I experienced it like an apocalyptic movie, so far removed from my actual reality that it didn't have the power to scare me. But then again, I didn't fear terrorists; I feared my ex-boyfriend breaking into my apartment, like he had done to my dorm the year before. I basically checked out, treating the first four Bush years like it was a stoner flick—by eating Chinese takeout and doubling over in laughter at presidential zingers like "I know the human being and fish can coexist peacefully."

I wasn't ready to engage with the world again until 2008, when at twenty-six, I finally registered to vote so I could support Barack Obama. I'd identified something in him that reminded me of my father. He was an intellectual with daughters who saw himself a citizen of the world. He was Ivy League educated but answered questions in a way anyone could understand. He used colloquialisms like "oughta" and "folks" and seemed genuinely interested in doing the right thing for people.

For election night, my father had given me a handwritten table of states and their corresponding number of electoral votes so I could tally them by hand, a tradition he'd started as a sixth-grader in 1960. When Obama won, I was elated. Finally, a president I felt proud of—and safe under. I hadn't been old enough to fully process Bill Clinton's presidency. I only knew my mother, who despised philanderers, referred to him as "Slick Willie."

For me, Obama was a complete departure. No scandal, no stupidity—just countless public displays of thoughtfulness. I trusted him so much that over eight years, a complacency cloud rolled in where the apathy had once lived. As reproductive rights were slowly being chipped away in conservative states, I did nothing. When Donald Trump, the antithesis of female empowerment, began his campaign, I thought no one would vote for him. I figured even if people weren't horrified by his actions or policies, at the very least they'd see he had primarily his own interests at heart. But I was the one who failed to see—he was precisely the kind of man they were looking for.

In Obama's first memoir, *Dreams from My Father,* published in 1995 when he was just thirty-four, he writes about what he learned as a community organizer:

> The self-interest I was supposed to be looking for extended well beyond the immediacy of issues, that beneath the small talk and sketchy biographies and received opinions, people carried with them some central explanation of themselves. Stories full of terror and wonder, studded with events that still haunted or inspired them. Sacred stories.

Having a president with the desire to scour the hearts and minds of the people was a privilege. It's part of what made the following election so traumatic—especially for those whose specters of terror bore any resemblance to the kind of hate incited by Donald Trump. I assumed Jack must have been thrilled by his victory, a fact later confirmed by his Facebook page.

When we dated twenty years ago, he introduced me to ethnic slurs I didn't even know existed. At the time, I attributed them to shoddy upbringing. I didn't understand that when any person is degraded, regarded as subhuman, that violence is an inevitable conclusion. My ignorance was a product of my privilege, both of which contributed to my complacency. This is not meant as an excuse so much as an admission. The same socioeconomic structures that protected me had failed him and countless others.

But money alone did not save me. When I was sixteen and dating Jack, I got pregnant and needed an abortion. Had I not been able to access that basic service and escape being tied to him for the rest of my life, I might not have had the opportunity to go to college, have a career, move away to a city, and live the life I thought I deserved.

In the fall of 1999, I sat in the cab of Jack's blue truck. I was seventeen with long, bottle-blonde hair just a few shades too yellow. He was crying; his pack of Marlboro Reds was leaning against a cupholder. The tears were real but the motivation behind them manufactured. He intended to manipulate me into not showing up for a court date. The state had pressed domestic battery charges against him on my behalf. Even though I'd fallen for him—the first person to love and comfort this new unlovable, uncomfortable teenage version of myself—I was able to determine the tears were a con job. Once he realized he'd lost control of me, his demeanor changed. He got a new girlfriend, yet continued to stalk me until he went to jail.

In order to dissect the situation afterward, even with years of buffering, I needed to separate myself from the events. Engaging in a post-mortem, an understanding of why this had happened, required me to have compassion—both for myself and for him. Cognitive empathy, understanding the reasons behind why people do things, and emotional empathy, feeling bad for them, are two different things. I can empathize with his life circumstances, the fact that he grew up in a pattern of severe family violence, substance abuse, and misogyny and still despise the belief systems that led to his actions. Similarly, we can empathize with the circumstances that lead others to make certain choices—and still oppose their language, policies, and rhetoric.

In politics, neither side cares to know the struggle of the other—we fear even the struggles within ourselves. Similarly, we avoid complicating the narratives we've already settled on, leaving the most difficult territory untrodden. I hadn't sought out stories about the people displaced and deported during the Obama administration or innocent civilians killed during drone attacks simply because I had already settled on a mythology about the man. Allowing oneself to become disillusioned with a system threatens the very belief structure propping it up. This is all to say that I don't believe any of us can move forward without acknowledging where we've failed.

The day my ex-boyfriend was scheduled to face a judge for his crimes against me, only my mother accompanied me to the courthouse. We were assured our presence would be enough to prompt a guilty plea and that I wouldn't have to set foot in the actual courtroom. My father was notably absent, working out of his second office two hours away. Perhaps he didn't know about the court date or only thought it had to do with the vandalism of our car. Or maybe my mother never told him. Back then, I still carried the shame of being a victim. I thought I had driven my boyfriend to hurt me, that I wasn't worthy of love. Only years later did it occur to me that my father really should have been there.

When I was thirty-three and living in New York City, my husband and I separated briefly. I was reckoning with all of the hurt from my past, and he had his own issues to overcome. At the time, I didn't know it would be temporary.

In the first week, my father, sixty-five and living with my mother in California, flew in to keep me company. I cried in his hotel room. I cried at his hotel gym. I laughed briefly as he pretended to struggle with tiny weights— then a giant sob overtook me again. I had taken time off of work to get my affairs in order, and my dad was like a friendly ghost in white tennis shoes and socks, khaki shorts, and a backpack, following me around the city in case I needed anything.

What I needed most was a distraction. But to have my sadness witnessed by my father, who supported me wholeheartedly and asked nothing in return, validated it somehow. His mere presence filled in part of my emptiness. All anyone really wants is to be seen and heard, and yet we avoid seeing and hearing others every day. Even among families, there are limits to what we can expect to receive from others. Sometimes we're left carrying our own stories, like oceans inside of us—pasts we cannot kill with neglect like some under-watered houseplant.

A week or so after my dad came to console me in New York City, I went to stay with my parents for a week in California. Emotions were rolling high, and my mother brought up the topic of my high school boyfriend, Jack. It was a wound in our family that had not healed, mostly because no one wanted to talk about it. The next day, after my father and I bought groceries, we were sitting in the Safeway parking lot, the sun beating down on the hood of his dark blue sports car.

"I didn't know he hit you," he said.

My mother had told him the night before. For some reason, I thought it was what had made him cry that time in my room. It had always made me feel worse—the idea that I had both caused my abuse and upset my dad in the process. In retrospect, he was probably just worried about me because he could actually imagine what kind of future I might be losing.

We traveled home in silence, the Pacific Ocean visible from the road. Tears fell from behind my tinted glasses, which had transition lenses, just like his. Although mine were a more fashionable pair, I'd chosen them in a kind of secret nerd solidarity.

Neither of us knew what to say.

THE ENDLESS CONTAINER

Fiona Apple once claimed that her work on *Tidal* was not the result of a highly publicized traumatic event she suffered earlier in life. "It doesn't get into the writing," she told *Q* magazine in 2000, about having been raped when she was just twelve. Apple was only responding to an inevitable question about the lyrics to "Sullen Girl," which were included in nearly every review of her 1996 debut, released when she was eighteen.

> *Is that why they call me a sullen girl, sullen girl*
> *They don't know I used to sail the deep and tranquil sea*
> *But he washed me 'shore*
> *And he took my pearl*
> *And left an empty shell of me*

You can't really blame her for wanting to distance her work from her trauma. A 1997 arts feature on Apple in the *New York Times* carried the headline, "A Message Far Less Pretty Than the Face." It's hard to imagine what it must have been like to be open about her rape in the 90s, especially having catapulted to fame so young. On her way home from school one day, a man had caught the door behind her as she was entering her mother's Manhattan apartment building. He cornered her in the corridor with a weapon and said if she screamed he'd kill her.

In 1998, she told *Rolling Stone* that she didn't think she would have achieved the same success if what happened to her had never occurred. She may have been right but not due to any lack of talent. Post-traumatic growth is known to open doors that otherwise would never appear—and to deepen an individual's ability to forge emotional connections. *Tidal* certainly resonated with an entire generation of young women who, like me, had no idea how to manage their own internal seas. Apple offered a safe place for us to store the unruliest of our emotions—sadness, anger, and jealousy.

> *And there's too much going on*
> *But it's calm under the waves*
> *In the blue of my oblivion*
> *Under the waves*
> *In the blue of my oblivion*

Billie Holiday, one of Apple's influences, was also raped—by a middle-aged neighbor in an abandoned house when she was just ten, an event for which she was imprisoned and later sent to reform school. She eventually turned to prostitution, alcohol, and heroin. In reference to her career, and specifically the song "Lady Sings the Blues," Maggie Nelson wrote, "To see blue in deeper and deeper saturation is eventually to move toward darkness."

Holiday and Apple can both be said to possess duende, a concept that is notoriously difficult to define, beyond the fact that it originates in Spain and describes an artistic soulfulness—often linked to darkness—which cannot be faked through any level of mastery or performance. In "Theory and Play of the Duende," a seminal work on the subject, the early 20th century poet, playwright, and director Federico García Lorca writes, "The great artists of

Southern Spain, Gypsy or flamenco, singers, dancers, musicians, know that emotion is impossible without the arrival of the duende."

In his essay, Lorca suggests that duende is not drawn from external forces such as style but rises from inside the artist—the blood itself. "The duende wounds," he explains, and "in trying to heal that wound that never heals, lies the strangeness, the inventiveness of a man's work." Apple's songs, as she once suggested, may not directly reference the past, but that doesn't mean the two aren't linked.

Some trauma theorists believe that the memory is not only etched in the mind, but also stored in the body. The cause of trauma is universally recognized as having witnessed or experienced events that involve the threat of death or serious bodily injury. This is where trauma and duende share a striking similarity; Lorca believed it would only appear if the artist has come face-to-face with the possibility of death.

He points out that in Spain, one needs look no further than the bullfight to understand death as a national spectacle—a performance. "At the moment of the kill, the aid of the duende is required to drive home the nail of artistic truth." We replicate a similar thrill by consuming art derived from trauma by experiencing another's suffering from a safe distance. As Lorca suggests, "Neither in Spanish dance nor in the bullfight does anyone enjoy himself: the duende charges itself with creating suffering by means of a drama of living forms, and clears the way for an escape from the reality that surrounds us."

The escape vessel produced by Apple's *Tidal* is twofold: the audience has both the opportunity to engage in what Carl Jung called *participation mystique*—sharing an identity and symbolic life with something outside of one's self—as well as a bit of healthy projection. I, too, participated in Apple's pain, while using her performance as a container for my own. Listening to *Tidal* as a teenager was a bit like pricking my own finger, then watching a tiny pool of blood give form to my feelings—the only safe way I knew to dip into the hurt.

"The *duende* never repeats itself, any more than the waves of the sea do in a storm," writes Lorca. An artist doesn't lose her soulfulness over time—she just finds new ways to express it. In the 1997 feature, "A Message Far Less Pretty Than the Face," Apple stated, post-*Tidal*, "I've already written new stuff and I have to let it out."

She seemed to be speaking to the struggle that duende is said to delight in with its creator, as if it were banging on a cage, begging to be released. Or maybe it's the other way around—the creator summoning her pain in an attempt to expunge it. Either way, the fire continues to burn, and Apple is the kindling. In *Bluets*, Maggie Nelson once called the blue flame at the core of a fire "an excellent example of how blue gives way to darkness—and then how, without warning, the darkness grows up into a cone of light."

This is perhaps the best metaphor I've found for duende and for art derived from trauma. The artist digs deep into her sadness to wrestle with its cause, which then surprises her with a kind of beauty—a light that could not be born of anything else. In keeping with the Spanish belief that death is merely another beginning, out of the ashes comes, as Lorca put it, "an endless baptism of freshly created things."

Apple has released four albums since her debut, in between hiatuses, to varying degrees of critical acclaim and commercial success. And though her writing has become more pointed and her style more refined, none has pierced me in quite the same way as *Tidal*. Her album was the first place my emotions felt acceptable, marking the beginning of what would become my own struggle with an indefinable force that seemed to be devouring me from the inside.

Twenty years later, I was quick to purchase *Tidal* upon its release on vinyl. When I listen to the record now, I do so not while driving a car with the sunroof open, the wind in my hair, a joint in hand—but on a leather couch, snuggled in a blanket, a few drops of CBD tincture under my tongue. As I fall into the blue of Apple's oblivion, time seems to suspend itself. I notice my feelings are no longer linked to any particular set of events. I can't be sure how much of the emotional intensity belongs to Apple and how much belongs to me—only that I never want the entwinement to end.

A WOMAN, A PLAN, AN OUTLINE OF A MAN

The solution came to me while watching the evening news: guns. I'd heard of people doing fire walks, beating pillows with baseball bats—even taking hallucinogens in the Peruvian rainforest. But I needed something more potent than an Amazonian shaman could provide.

At twenty-three I was raped. Fresh out of college, I had no idea what I wanted to do with my life, which at the time revolved around working a few shifts a week as a bartender, going out afterward—and debating whether I had enough money left over at the end of the month to buy those discounted designer shoes (the answer, true or not, was always yes).

One night, I went to the apartment of guy I knew from work to smoke a joint and listen to music. I only liked him as a friend, but I let him kiss me anyway. He lived in a studio, and I decided to take a quick nap before attempting to drive home. I didn't worry about being raped by someone I knew. Why would you?

When I awoke, I found he had unzipped my pants and stuck his fingers inside of me. I froze. He kept going. While it was happening, my mind completely checked out. Afterward, I told myself it had all been a big misunderstanding—because that was simply easier than confronting the truth.

My denial allowed me to ignore the panic attacks I suffered over the next ten years. Even now, as a thirty-three-year-old woman living in a different city with a successful career, the hair on the back of my neck still stood up whenever I was in my office building's elevator alone with a group of men.

And yet, pretending like it never happened worked so well for so long. I didn't even wonder why I hadn't gone on a date for almost a decade. Instead, I had two long-term relationships with men who had both been my friends. I married the second.

He became the first person I ever told—and only because I felt I owed him an explanation after bursting into tears during sex.

"I was raped."

The words just fell out of my mouth.

"I'm sorry that happened to you," he responded.

I wasn't willing to discuss the details—I found them too painful. And he didn't push me. Eventually, I went to see a therapist for my chronic anxiety. When she asked if I'd ever been sexually assaulted, I offered only a "maybe." Still, it took a whole year for me to tell her what exactly had happened.

Talking about it was like draining an infected wound. And after several months, I saw the first flaky signs of a scab—in the form of anger.

The original twinges arrived by way of violent revenge fantasies. Like the flashbacks I'd experienced when I first started talking about my sexual assault in therapy, they crept in from uncharted corners of my mind. I found myself picturing my rapist's head—except it was no longer attached to his body. Having been violated in such a personal and irreversible manner, I wanted to somehow do the same to him. Also, I happened to be binge-watching *The Walking Dead*.

Actual, non-zombie violence still repelled me, but the idea of make-believe revenge had a disparate appeal. When my anger finally presented itself, channeling it seemed the only viable escape from a deep sadness. Now that I knew my wound had the power to heal, I wanted to pick at the scab— and relish in my newfound ability to bleed.

I would have never even considered guns had they not been constantly popping up in my Facebook feed between photos of my baby nieces at a pumpkin patch and family portraits of people I barely knew in high school. The stream was unrelenting: article shares, status updates, and daily comments. Guns had become so embedded in our culture I was almost surprised curiosity hadn't gotten the better of me sooner.

Sure, a kickboxing or self-defense class may have offered a similar release, but what I really wanted was access to something I felt had been taken from me when I experienced rape. As a young liberal living in city with strict gun laws, it had never occurred to me that there might be people attending target practice just a block away from my office on Fifth Avenue. A quick Google search revealed the only shooting range in Manhattan happened to be down the street from where I'd been working as a copywriter for three years at a women's fashion brand.

I imagined myself presenting snappy headlines about this season's Italian cashmere in the morning, firing off a few rounds over lunch, and then returning in time for my afternoon e-commerce connection meeting. I thought if I took on a new secret—like leading a double life as a markswoman—it might somehow override the shameful one that had lived inside of me for so many years.

The range required I pass a background check and attend a short safety lesson before I could handle a .22-caliber rifle. The laws in NYC restrict citizens from even renting a handgun without a license—a disappointment for my fantasy, which had me in red lipstick and leather pants, my legs hip-width apart as I fired bullets out of a silver pistol and into the heart of a shadowy male figure.

Instead, I wore jeans and a sweater and recruited my husband to tag along.

"But you hate guns," he said.

He had a point. After the shooting in Sandy Hook that took the lives of twenty children and six adults, guns went from a danger to society to downright detestable, in my mind. If owning a firearm led to either nothing or death, why take the risk? As a proponent of animal rights, I also despised hunting. When confronted with a spider of almost any size, my response was usually a high-pitched squeak followed by, "Don't kill it!"

I'd never even seen a gun up close but suddenly couldn't wait to get my hands on one—if only in a desperate attempt to reclaim something I'd lost. I scheduled our safety session for the next available Saturday, and we arrived fifteen minutes early to a basement on 20th Street lined with photos of gun-wielding celebrities like 50 Cent and Robert De Niro. A group of mustached men sat near the check-in window discussing Texas's open carry laws, their sentences punctuated by loud popping noises from the shooting range.

"Rifle lesson?" one asked.

He pointed us toward a classroom that reminded me of middle-school detention, except with weapons training. The first thing we did was sign releases stating that we understood our visits might result in death.

Fine, whatever—get to the guns. My hyperactive safety instincts tried to kick in, but I kicked them straight back out, only momentarily picturing what my parents' reactions to the news of my untimely death might be.

A man with full-sleeve tattoos and Vans slip-ons gave a twenty-minute demo, during which I learned how to load my weapon, operate the safety, and probably avoid accidentally shooting anyone. The experience was surreal—grasping the basics of handling a firearm alongside four other couples who would appear less out of place squabbling over thread count in the bedding department at Macy's.

Next, we moved on to filling our magazines, which I learned meant shoving bullets into little plastic containers that looked like powder-keg Monopoly hotels. I was nervously lining mine up along the table when I noticed our instructor setting up the lanes with standard archery targets. I raised my hand to ask the goblin tattoo on his neck a question.

"Is there any way I could shoot at the outline of a person?"

This felt important to my healing process.

He disappeared into an office and reappeared with a stack of shaded-in male figures. "Take as many as you like."

I needed only one, which I clipped to the cord above my shooting booth and wound out into my lane about twenty-five feet. I loaded the first rounds into my rifle, set my line of sight at the center of the silhouette, braced myself, and pulled the trigger. Nothing happened. *Oops—safety*. I clicked the switch to red ("red=dead," I'd learned in the lesson), refocused my aim, and then pulled the trigger again.

The bullet went straight through my target's neck.

Freeing oneself from blame after a rape is like facing the inevitability of death. First, you have to accept the absence of any thread connecting you to an alternate universe in which you may have had access to a different fate. For me, that thread was spun from fibers like "I didn't have to drink that night," "I didn't have to go into his apartment," and certainly "I didn't have to kiss him." Fear of whatever grief might reveal itself once that thread finally snapped was precisely what kept it in place.

Shortly after my original lifeline of denial and Xanax broke, I found myself grasping for any proof that I could have somehow prevented what happened. Only when I let go of the self-blame was I able to let in the anger. It washed over me like a torrent. I suddenly wanted to scream at every person I passed on the street. I was angry my life had been forever changed for reasons I would never understand. I was angry that for years, instead of hating the person responsible, I'd actually hated myself. I was even angry that I hadn't gotten angry sooner.

I had falsely assumed shooting would work out for me like bowling or darts—that is, poorly—so I was surprised when I was able to hit my target at all, let alone fifty times through the chest. *Who's incapacitated now?* It felt oddly serene, looking down the barrel of a rifle while holding my body as still as possible and calmly pumping out a round per second.

I was interrupted only when the gun jammed—if a bullet loaded incorrectly or a shell casing failed to expel properly. By the time I'd ripped through all of my allotted ammo, there were two extra bullets from failed attempts. I pocketed them as souvenirs and swept up the brass casings from the floor.

I decided then to check in on my husband in the next booth over, who seemed to have forgotten why we were there in the first place. He was gleefully pulling the trigger on something called a bolt-action rifle, which had a slower fire rate, and was taking longer to unload all of his ammunition.

He had to manually pull a lever (the bolt action) before each shot, which caused the gun to kick back into his shoulder. It released .38-caliber bullets, which blew visibly larger holes in his circular target than my .22s, which suddenly appeared puny by comparison.

I decided I wasn't quite ready to go home either. Perhaps I feared my anger would be fleeting—that if I let my rage slip away, I would fall back into sadness. Or maybe I was even more afraid that I might get better. That one day I would move on with my life and no longer wonder if the man who raped me had a wife or a daughter or if he even remembered my name.

I went back to my shooting booth and pulled out the bullets I'd saved in my pocket. I pressed them into one of my empty magazines, slammed it into the chamber of my rifle, and shot the paper silhouette twice more through the chest.

When I originally suggested the shooting range to my husband as an outlet for my healing, I had been attending twelve-week group therapy for sexual assault survivors. In the first session, a woman said something that stuck with me. She felt like a piece of her soul had been stolen from her and hidden at the bottom of the ocean—and that no matter what she did, she would never be able to find it or get it back.

Over the next weeks, we all were asked to share the details of our assaults. When I told my own story, I thought I might die from shame. But when I heard what had happened to the other women, I became angry on their behalf. When they expressed feelings of self-blame, I felt empathy—they were clearly not to blame. Over time, I learned something important: neither was I.

When we talked about how to move on with our lives, one woman said to the first woman:

"You're like a phoenix, rising from the ashes."

This made me wonder what my own life could have been like had it never been reduced to ashes.

There is a certain finality that comes with having shot a gun. You cannot unlearn how easy it would be to actually hurt someone. You remember that nothing in life can be truly taken back.

I didn't return to the range in the next few weeks, although I considered it. I kept my shiny new three-month membership card in the outside pocket of my leather backpack next to my keys, secretly hoping it would fall out while I was mid-conversation with a friend or colleague.

Oops, I imagined myself saying, blushing as I leaned over to pick up the card from Westside Rifle & Pistol with my name on it.

Maybe what I really wanted was a reason to tell people why I'd taken up shooting in the first place so they would understand I was mourning something real. I had lost someone—the version of myself who had not been raped, the person I could have been for the past ten years, a young woman who felt safe in the world. This is the kind of grief you don't just drop casually into conversation. Sexual assault makes others uncomfortable, which is part of why surviving one can feel so isolating.

Guns, on the other hand, are somehow fair game. So I sat at home on a Saturday, scrolling through photos my husband had taken of me at the range while I unwittingly focused on my posture and aim. I picked my favorite— one of me in pink noise protector earmuffs, rifle in hand—and texted it to a close friend with the caption *channeling my rage*. Next, I sent her one of my target, which had been shredded by the tiny bullets. I had to admit, it looked good.

STUCK IN A WATER WELL

Every little girl deserves her own elephant. I got mine when I was six. It was the biggest stuffed version of Dumbo that Disney World had to offer. At nearly a foot and a half tall, the little guy was half my size. His blue cap and white collar complemented the pink lining of his soft ears. He sat in a permanently fixed position on his hind legs as I—a little blonde girl in striped pajamas—threw my arms around his neck. The one flaw in my elephant's design—how stiff his arms were. No matter how I tried, he could not hug me back.

To be fair, I already had what amounted to a herd of huggable stuffed animals that lived in a heaping pile on my bed. My menagerie was flush with smaller elephants but also included dogs, marine mammals, and one raccoon puppet my family called Rocky. Their soft, plush bodies kept me company as I drifted off to sleep each night—a plastic eye jabbing me in the shoulder blade or forearm as my tiny body tossed and turned. I had separation anxiety as a child, which manifested itself in the form of nightmares, but I wasn't allowed to wake up my parents.

My dad was an ophthalmologist who worked long hours sticking things in people's eyes. He needed to be at peak performance, which meant he needed to sleep, lest he have a cataract surgery to perform the next morning.

"Go to bed," my mother would scold if I came into their room in the middle of the night. She stayed home from work when I was a kid—rather reluctantly, it seemed—and by the time I was in junior high, she'd gone back part-time.

My animal friends comforted me in way I didn't fully understand—at least not until I witnessed a similar phenomenon as an adult. For a year, I volunteered at an animal shelter in lower Manhattan that had about twenty rescue dogs in a basement. After work, I dropped by to take them out for walks and mop up the larger dogs' enclosures. I had to coax the smaller dogs—the Maltese, the Yorkies, the Chihuahuas—out with kind words before wiping out their kennels behind them by hand. When one dog would start barking, the others inevitably joined in.

"That's why we have them all on doggie Prozac," one of the staffers told me.

"What's doggie Prozac?"

"Regular Prozac," she said. "Just in a lower dose."

One of the larger dogs seemed particularly sad. Her sable, furry body covered nearly three quarters of the width of her enclosure. When the others started howling, she didn't even lift her head. One night, I saw her holding a stuffed bear in her paws. She had positioned its feet under one of her arms and its head propped up on the other, as if she wanted to be able to see its face. I had to take the little bear from her, so she wouldn't ingest any part of it during the night. When I saw the look in her glassy brown eyes as I did this, I couldn't help but think I must have been a very lonely little girl.

In my thirties, I got a second life-size elephant—this time via the internet. My husband and I had flown to spend Christmas at my parents' house in Northern California, where they had retired. We didn't have children, but they still wanted to give us the illusion of the family holiday, including a fully decorated tree and presents. My mother handed me a red envelope, which I promptly ripped open. The card read, *For our sweet animal-loving daughter*. Inside was a printout of the photo of an elephant orphan my parents had "fostered" me as a Christmas gift. Her name was Suswa.

"Her name is just like mine," she said.

My mother's name is Susan. She'd sent me an email a month before asking what I wanted for Christmas. I responded that I didn't need anything, but when she pressed me on it, I forwarded her a link to a charity that operates an elephant rescue in Kenya. For $50, my parents could sponsor me a baby elephant, many of whom had been orphaned by the ivory trade.

"Do you want to pick one?" she asked.

I had already taken a gander at the orphan profiles, but by the third, my eyes stung with tears and I had to close my browser. *Lemoyian. He fell down a man-made well and got separated from his family. Mashariki. Found on her own, weak and near collapse. Lualeni. She was found abandoned and, despite trying to join other herds, seemed to be rejected by all.*

"You can pick," I answered.

I assumed she would select one of the nursery babies because they were adorable. One even wore a pink blanket and drank milk formula out of a bottle directly from the keeper's hands. But my mother didn't choose a baby elephant from the nursery. Instead, she selected a 5-year-old that had been rescued a few years back and was now categorized as an "older and adolescent orphan" by the organization's website.

"Look at her pretty blanket," she said as we sat on the floor in front of the fireplace. In the photo that came with my card, Suswa was only eighteen months and had just been rescued. She wore a red and orange blanket typical of Maasai tribesman. It covered her back and fell halfway down her sides. Her ears were spread straight out, her posture cautiously assertive—chin up, one foot slightly forward.

Suswa. Found on her own, extremely wild and fearful.

My own older and adolescent years were a disaster for the already tenuous relationship I had with my mother. As I explored new methods of easing my ever present anxiety—drinking, smoking pot, and sneaking out—my mother grew less and less patient with me.

Once when I was fifteen, I came home drunk. Okay, many times when I was fifteen, I came home drunk. But this particular time still haunts me because my mother was there to greet me in the front yard. She grabbed my wrist and smelled my breath.

"You've been drinking!" she said.

She then latched onto my arm roughly, but I resisted. I fought her off until she was just holding me by the sleeve. So I slipped out of my shirt and ran away—wearing only a black and red satin bra from Victoria's Secret. I ran four or five blocks through the pitch-black suburban night, my skin piercing the humid air. I didn't know what to do, so I went to a friend's house. I knew his room was on the ground floor. When I approached the window, I could see him watching TV inside. I knocked.

"Do you have an extra shirt?"

He gave me one, and I hid out there until morning. By then the alcohol had worn off, and I was even more afraid of going back home to face my mother.

After my tumultuous teenage years passed, my mother and I never resolved our conflicts. Instead we spoke in a language that relied on omission and vague references. We avoided and ignored, choosing instead to talk only about my childhood, before things got rocky—when I was still a cute little girl who loved elephants.

The January after I became a proud elephant foster parent, I began receiving a monthly email update from the wildlife trust with news about the orphans. It included a Keeper's Diary, which I could search by Suswa's name to browse text entries and photos that included her. I followed the links to find images of elephants drinking from a watering hole and frolicking in the clay-colored mud, sometimes lying on their sides with their legs sticking straight out. They seemed like a boisterous bunch.

The orphans downed their morning milk bottle before beginning a game of chasing one another around the compound. Tundani was bumper to bumper trying to mount anyone while Nelion returned to the stockades to scratch his itchy buttocks against the metal posts. Suswa was very affectionate toward her best friend, Arruba, greeting her warmly and resting her trunk on Arruba's back.

I was happy to learn Suswa had a friend. Since her rescue, she had been moved from the nursery to a re-integration unit in Tsavo National Park, Kenya, where older orphans could roam freely throughout the day and still have a place to sleep at night, safe from predators.

Elephants communicate via a complex language, which includes infrasonic calls they can detect through their feet over a mile away, rumbling noises like bellows and trumpets, nonverbal cues such as ear flapping and trunk gesturing, as well as direct touch. When one elephant feels insecure, another will put its trunk in his or her mouth—the equivalent to handholding in human society.

Even at five-and-a-half years old, Suswa was already beginning to fraternize with older ex-orphans who had rejoined wild herds, learning the social skills she would need to eventually do the same. It would take eight to ten years in total for her to return to the wild, and even then, she would likely keep in touch with her human families. Ex-orphans had been observed returning to the facility for medical treatment and even to introduce newborn babies to their former keepers. The lifelong, close-knit bonds found in elephant society mimic those of our own—or, at least, the way we are at our best.

When I first left home at eighteen for college, which was only an hour away, my mother and I spoke on the phone about once a week. She'd ask how school was going, what I was learning in my classes, when was I coming home to do laundry. But over the next decade, our correspondence lessened. She retreated into her new life as a retiree, and I into mine as a young woman trying to find her footing in life.

That is, until my older sister had her first baby. Suddenly my mother was a Facebook grandma-at-large. She bought her first laptop and took trips to the Apple store every month to learn how to use the programs—her main objective being to edit and store photos of her grandchild so she could post them a few times a week.

"How do you attach a photo?" she once called to ask me so she could email me one of my niece. She then sent me a photograph of her six-month-old granddaughter, smiling in a stroller, a pink sun hat shading her face.

"Cute!" I said, in the way one responds to such an email.

When I did talk to her on the phone, she never told me anything of much significance. Instead, she would drone on about the banalities of her day. What she bought at the store and why. Who she played tennis with.

Did I see that new baby pic she posted?

"Um-huh," I'd say, just listening to the lull of her voice, the cadence of her sentences. It reminded me of listening to her talk on the phone as a girl. The sound was just comforting enough to put me to sleep, but the soothing stopped there—she was impenetrable should I ever wake up and need something more. In February, my husband and I began planning our annual vacation, which we usually do in the dead of winter to boost morale. Not having children has its perks when it comes to traveling—we can go anywhere pretty much anytime, so long as we can produce the cash.

For me, the lack of desire to have a baby could be traced all the way back to my herd of stuffed animals, which I much preferred to faux mini-humans. As an adult, the preference held with their real-life counterparts.

"What about going to the elephant nursery?" I asked my husband. "It's in Nairobi."

"We could go on a safari," he suggested.

We ended up finding a company in the Maasai Mara, a famous national park and wildlife reserve in Kenya. Twice a year, enormous herds of wildebeest and zebra pass through it during their migration. It is also the park where Suswa was rescued. I wouldn't see her there or in Nairobi, since she'd been moved to the reintegration unit, but I would get to see some of the other orphans. When it came time to buy the flights, I started to get cold feet, a condition that manifested itself in various, semi-valid safety concerns, which I voiced in rapid succession over dinner one evening.

"What about the lion that jumped through the window and killed that lady?" I asked my husband suddenly. I'd seen the story on the news about a year before.

"That was at, like, a zoo."

"And Al-Shabaab?"

"We'll stay in a safe hotel."

"What about malaria?"

"You can take pills before you go."

This was really just a distraction from what I was most afraid of: seeing the orphans in person. Having to face precisely how horribly humankind had failed the elephant species would perhaps be too much for me. Once I saw on television a baby elephant being removed from a sewer grate in India. Though she survived with only a broken foot, I squealed as they were pulling her out. Even as an adult, when I watch the scene in Dumbo where he goes to visit his mother in the circus-imposed jail, I can't help but sob uncontrollably.

Maybe it's the elephants themselves—how caring they are with one another. Why can't humans treat each other—and them—with the same tenderness? Instead, men with AR-15s shoot them from airplanes so they can sell their teeth for trinkets.

Elephant society is matriarchal, and the babies are dependent on their mothers' milk for up to three years. Calves also rely on a cadre of aunts and siblings, whose comforting trunks are never farther than a few paces away. But in the end, elephant families operate as a single organism, which means at some point, they must move on for the sake of the herd, if one member is sick—or even if a little calf is stuck in a water well.

Some of the most difficult times I've been through in my life, I've been through with limited support from my mother. This has been, in part, my choice, carried out as a means of self-protection. I feared if I showed too much of myself, she might reject me.

Once, the summer before she "adopted" me Suswa, I told her that in order for us to have a real relationship as adults, we'd need to actually talk about the things that had happened when I was a girl—situations she'd failed to recognize, help me with, or take responsibility for her part in, like when we fought a lot during high school and I sought refuge in what turned out to be an abusive relationship, or when she confiscated my birth control and I got pregnant not long after.

"Let's leave it in the past," she said.

When I kept pushing her, I realized she was still angry with me—for what I wasn't sure. Being a difficult teenager? An emotionally needy child? Sometimes I think the elephant orphans might wonder forever what was wrong with them that drove their mothers away. Elephants never forget a face, and when they're united with a long-lost companion, they demonstrate an emotional response. Liquid leaks from temporal glands near their ears—a stress response akin to human tears.

My mother and I live on opposite coasts, so we see each other fairly infrequently. A few years ago, I bought a book called *Mothering and Daughtering* and told her about it during one of our visits. She immediately changed the subject. The book was about keeping the bond strong through the teenage years and beyond, which is really where our relationship had left off. When she dismissed me, I could almost see it there, hanging limply like a frayed cord. I never read the book. Instead, I moved it to the lowest level of my bookshelf and chastised myself for being so stupid.

In March, I received via email my updated Keeper's Diary for Foster Parents, which highlighted a newer orphan.

We have a young girl called Roi in our midst who has become increasingly mischievous and has recently developed a new trick. Without the keepers being aware, she has worked out how to surreptitiously sneak an extra bottle of milk from the wheelbarrow, thereafter rushing close to the visiting public at the cordon for protection whilst rapidly gulping down the contents before tossing the bottle aside.

I immediately liked Roi and decided to read more about her. In the process, I learned a tourist had photographed her in the Maasai Mara, where we were planning to go on safari, happily feeding from her mother. But the next day, he returned to find the little calf grief-stricken. Her mother had been killed by a poisonous dart, and her gigantic corpse now lay at the little elephant's feet. At ten months, Roi was milk-dependent and wouldn't survive alone with the herd. She would only grow weaker and weaker until they were forced to leave her behind.

I couldn't bring myself to watch the video of her rescue. *Roi. Found next to her dead mother in the company of the rest of her herd.*

As my own mother aged, I became less inclined to rock the boat with my emotional needs. She seemed to be steadily morphing into a miniature version of the imposing figure I once remembered—her shoulders sloping, her hair almost entirely silver. I, too, had aged. Tiny wrinkles sprouted from the outer corners of my eyes.

I began to see my mother less as someone to fear and more as a person with flaws—imperfect, like me. And though I couldn't pretend to know what it was like to have a child of my own, I understood her reluctance to engage with me in the way I wanted. To love someone fully means to hurt when they hurt—and to acknowledge where you've failed them. It's a surrender of sorts, which can be an uncomfortable act for anyone.

I know it's not the same thing, but when the Sarah McLachlan shelter-dog commercial comes on, my impulse is to change the channel immediately. Animals, not humans, have always brought out my soft side. It pains me to watch videos of rescuers loading tranquilized baby elephants onto tarp-covered mattresses—carrying them away from the only place they'd ever known as home, even though I know it's their sole chance at survival. But I do know from my own recovery process that if you don't allow yourself to bear witness, to feel the lowest of the lows, you restrict your own access to the highs.

The little calves, frightened and weak, are often near collapse upon capture and have only sparse layers of fuzz to keep them warm. When they get to the nursery, they can barely walk but are soon found eagerly accepting milk from a bottle. By the end of the videos, they're trotting full-strength through the shrubbery on their way to the watering hole to douse themselves in mud.

The following November, in 2016, I summoned the strength to try again with my mother. I had recently published an essay about surviving the sexual assault in my early twenties, which I posted to Facebook. I hadn't told my mother about the assault until earlier that year, and although she'd been supportive, we hadn't spoken about it since. I'd written about my experience publicly before but given her permission not to read it because I knew it would make her uncomfortable.

This time, I couldn't do that again, so I texted her an image of Dumbo the baby elephant with his giant ears spread out, eyes wide at the world around him. I told her it hurt me that she was unable to acknowledge the traumatic experiences from my past—and I needed to know she could witness my recovery and not have to look away.

I cried while typing this into my iPhone.

She emailed me in response to tell me she loved me, and she was sorry that I had to endure her bad mothering. I hadn't meant to hurt my mother—or cast blame on her for the ways the world had hurt me. I only wanted her to be able to see me in all of my ugliness and love me anyway, like Dumbo's mother had loved him. In the movie, she spanks a little boy for taunting her baby and pulling on his unusually large ears—a crime which contributes to her later being put into solitary confinement. When Dumbo discovers his unsightly ears have given him the gift of flight, he quickly becomes the star of the circus. What was once his greatest shame ends up setting them both free.

At the time, I felt my own greatest shame becoming my superpower, giving me access to a level of empathy that hadn't been there before—an ability to feel things I didn't know existed. I was finally setting myself free by expanding my emotional capacity and experiencing empathy in entirely new ways. I was learning to love, and I didn't want to leave my mother behind.

At dusk in Nairobi National Park, warthogs scurried back and forth around a muddy camp that housed upwards of thirty elephant orphans, a giraffe named Kiko, and a blind rhino named Maxwell. Each resident had his or her own custom living space with a hand-carved wooden sign hanging next to the door. Many of the names were familiar to me from the monthly newsletters. *Esampu. Ndotto. Roi.*

My husband and I stood in a clearing, where a well-worn path met the forest, as two iridescent cobalt dung beetles worked in tandem on a ping pong ball-sized prize. In the distance, we could see the first mud-colored head trotting toward us. When a keeper in a green rain slicker began reading off their name and ages, we realized the elephants were coming home single-file, smallest to largest.

I recognized some of the babies from the online diary with blankets still on their backs for security and warmth. They passed us, trunks flailing, and continued toward their little homes for feeding time with the keepers. I noticed that Roi—now in the back of the line at two years old—appeared gigantic when compared to the newcomers. Tiny tusks pushed up around her trunk. Once inside of her stockade, she polished off a pile of fresh greens while shifting her weight back and forth on her stocky legs.

Human keepers were assigned to stay overnight with the infants in indoor stables. They had elevated bunks with blankets hanging down—to mimic the physical presence of a mother elephant. When the babies' tiny trunks weren't busy stuffing leaves in their mouths or reaching through a fence to steal hay from an unsuspecting neighbor, they were reaching for their keepers and sometimes even sniffing out a visiting foster parent like me.

One of the littlest calves, Esampu, grew sleepy in her stable after dinner and began to sway back and forth. Her keeper was readying what looked like an exercise mat for her to sleep on amongst the hay, where she would remain visible from the bunk above. But the little calf was already shutting her eyes and toppled over in the opposite direction. The keeper sighed as he tried to drag the three-hundred-pound baby onto the mat without any luck. She was out cold.

"Sometimes they just don't land where you want them to," he said.

I watched her sleep for a minute or so before moving on to the next stable where a similar scene was playing out. Soon it grew dark, and the nursery was closing to visitors. My husband and I shuttled back to our hotel, removed our muddy shoes, took showers, and crawled into bed. Inside of me, the little girl who loved Dumbo cried tears of joy.

EVERYONE GETS A DOG

I found my soft, shiny stuffed dog on a tree of puppets at a souvenir shop in Big Sur. He was the color of asphalt, with glossy plastic eyes that disappeared under his dark fur and floppy ears that made him look more like a bunny than a black Lab. His rear end was plump and his tail thick. Through an opening in his chest, you could slip your hand inside. The feeling was intimate, like reaching into a shirt when one of the buttons has been undone.

The first time I did this, he came alive, opening his mouth to show off his pink tongue. I asked if he wanted to come home with me, and he nodded, his tail wagging from the flicker of my fingers. When I scratched behind his ears, he lifted his head as if he were relishing in the feeling.

"What should we call him?" I asked my husband.

"Blackberry," he said.

I found the name quite charming. As we drove away, my dog puppet stuck his head out the window, enjoying the salty air and sweeping seaside views.

While we were visiting my parents in California, Blackberry seemed nothing more than a silly indulgence. But once we got back to New York, I found myself spending more time with him than I would have a beloved stuffed animal from childhood. Pretending to feed him dog food. Making him lick and bite his front paws. Forcing him to chase his tail. I found it relaxing and enjoyable. Others found it a bit strange.

Although studies have shown up to forty percent of adults still sleep with stuffed animals, whether it's normal for a thirty-five-year-old woman to play with one daily does not seem to be part of mainstream scientific inquiry. Add the puppetry element into the mix (absent, of course, an audience), and people are bound to get a little weirded out.

One friend asked what it was exactly that I did with Blackberry.

"He delivers messages around the house," I said. "Like, *What's for dinner?!*"

To be fair, there are only two people around the house, my husband and me, and our house is really just a 500-square-foot apartment.

"He also likes to sing and dance," I added, hoping it would make my predilection more palatable.

"Uh-huh," she said, still skeptical.

As a child I used my whole herd of stuffed animals as a body pillow as I lay in bed reading books—my own private safari escape. It had always been my dream for them to one day come alive and gain the ability to speak. When I offered this as an explanation for my new stuffed animal puppet acquisition to my father, he summarily dismissed me suggesting even if they had come alive, they probably wouldn't have had anything interesting to say.

"Sarah," he said, in the imaginary baritone of a teddy bear. "Turn off the light."

Once, when my sister was visiting, I sat on my gray leather sofa anxiously petting Blackberry, using him as a sort of therapy dog.

"He's nervous," I told her before putting the hand not inside of him up to my mouth and whispering toward her ear, "that means I'm nervous."

"Yeah, I got it," she said.

I found the act of petting Blackberry to be soothing in two senses: I was both the one offering comfort and the one receiving it (me being also inside of the puppet). Does the act of nurturing not also nurture the nurturer? When I tried to explain the profundity of this dynamic to my husband, he said I was completely overthinking it.

"You just like to be constantly entertained," he said, "so you don't have to be alone with your thoughts." Having very few friends, I had always thought aloneness was a problem for extroverts. I believed, with an air of judgment, those who kept their social schedules packed did so to avoid being alone. Introverts, I now see, have the same problem; we just have greater incentive to adapt—and more time to develop our coping skills.

When I got Blackberry, I had a husband I loved, a job I liked, and no plans for children. But I still felt something was missing from my life. I decided to make a vision board, a collage of images representing various areas of my life (love, intellectual fulfillment, health). I thought if I stared at it long enough, a solution to my problem would present itself—my problem being nothing more than an indefinable sense of longing.

On the board, I'd cut out and pasted an image of an older woman, a wildlife conservationist, tenderly putting her hand to the cheek of a baby elephant orphan. When I carefully applied the printout using a glue stick, I meant it to symbolize alternative motherhood. But while staring at the photo, I began to think I identified more with the alternative child. There was something familiar about the little elephant's position. Have we not all felt alone in the world, helpless and in need of a tender hand? In need of a caregiver who could love us even more unconditionally than a pet—one who asked for nothing in return but our happiness?

At the time, I couldn't have had a pet if I wanted to. I worked all day, and my husband had allergies. I looked into buying a cat robot meant to act as emotional support for the elderly. It blinked and meowed and rolled onto its back so you could rub its tummy. I'd also considered the Japanese robot Paro, which looks like an adorable stuffed harp seal but is actually a $5,000 therapeutic assistance tool for dementia patients.

A friend who knew of my interests sent me a link to a Kickstarter where I could order a headless furry mound with a tail that wagged when you petted it. The marketing copy on their website read "Stroke, React, Get Healed" and showed a sad looking Japanese woman petting the mound and watching it wag its tail in response, although the extent to which she "got healed" and the scope of what ailed her remained unclear. The device wasn't available until the following year, and I wasn't sure about owning a wagging headless pillow, so I settled on a second dog puppet—which was essentially, I realized later, a pillow with a head and tail I could operate myself.

I ordered the yellow-Lab model of Blackberry from Amazon and named him Waffles. He had front legs you could operate with your thumb and pinky (Blackberry's were stuffed and almost impossible to animate). Waffles used his front legs to clap when he was having fun, pretend to conduct an orchestra, and occasionally attempt to close my husband's eyelids, as if he were gently ushering a newly deceased corpse toward its final resting place. When I played with both dogs at the same time, I called it "Dog Mittens." They were like two furry potholders with plastic eyes and black leather noses. Sometimes I made them French kiss and then felt bad about it, like I was some kind of puppet pedophile.

By obsessively searching online for other people who might like dog puppets, I discovered that if I were a fetishist, I could use them for some very dark purposes. As it turns out, I am just an enthusiast, along the lines of stuffed animal collectors and hoarders who attend Furry conventions but leave their loved ones at home for fear of being mistaken as perverts. When I asked my husband if he thought I might be a non-sexual plushophile, he said I was reading too deeply into this whole thing.

I disagreed with his assessment. My dog puppets had become a significant part of my home life, and I wanted to understand why. They served as part pet, part entertainment, and part mental health apparatus—an analog version of the therapeutic robots I'd discovered online.

At the time, I'd been seeing a therapist for two years for anxiety. But once, I noticed on the invoice she'd listed my condition as dysthymia— persistent depressive disorder. It was the first I'd heard of PDD, which is like depression but with less severe and longer-lasting symptoms. Sufferers of this type of melancholy may experience feeling hopeless and empty, but they think it's just a part of their character. The symptoms, which include avoiding social activities, were forming an outline of a woman I recognized—a woman who stayed home and played with her puppet.

Maybe my indefinable longing was a chemical imbalance, and my puppets were helping me through a rough time. Maybe this was all totally normal and fine. Maybe it was even something worth celebrating. At least, that's how I found myself addressing imaginary critics. Deep down, I must have thought there was something fundamentally wrong with me, or I wouldn't have constantly searched for an explanation as to why I played Dog Mittens every night—beyond the simple fact that it brought me joy.

One limitation of using a stuffed animal puppet as your DIY care-bot, I learned, besides making your arm tired, is that it can only love you as unconditionally as you love yourself. But an advantage is that a puppet is actually capable of love, as opposed to just a programmed sequence of behaviors meant to imitate it.

I was lying in bed with Blackberry one night when he lifted his head, turned it straight toward me, and said, "I love you, Mama."

The declaration startled me. I had no idea I was capable of such an expression of gentleness toward myself.

"I love you too," I told him.

Later, when I casually mentioned this to my therapist, she suggested I bring him to a session. I could never settle on a good time to pack Blackberry into a bag, take him on the subway, and keep him at work all day, so I put it off. I thought he might get dirty or stolen or I would have an uncontrollable urge to play with him at the office. Plus, traveling with a stuffed animal gave me anxiety. It reminded me of losing a beloved comfort object as a child—the moment I realized I'd left Rodney the Reindeer in the taxi, and Christmas would never be the same.

Being fairly attached to Blackberry, I also worried about how I would feel if my therapist reacted to him in the wrong way. Once I'd brought a large stuffed panda I'd gotten for Christmas from my husband, complete with a big red bow, to my parents' house for the holidays. I celebrated by tossing him up into the air and spinning around in a circle below.

"Well, this is new," my mother said dryly, before continuing on with her crossword puzzle.

My therapist practiced AEDP, a type of psychotherapy that aims to find untapped reservoirs of strength within subjects so they may draw upon them to deal with difficult feelings. The practice is centered on the idea of "undoing aloneness." It encourages a safe space for subjects to experience all of their emotions and embody their most authentic selves.

Perhaps my therapist could sense that my most authentic self had at some point been repressed and that my untapped resource could be tapped by covering one of my hands with a furry sock in the shape of a Lab puppy.

It actually took a few months to ready myself emotionally for puppet therapy. That morning on the subway, I noticed a man peering into my tote bag. Blackberry has a fairly realistically shaped body—the advantage, I think, of the stuffed animal-puppet hybrid model over one that looks like it could be a cover for a nine iron. I put my hand firmly over the outside of my bag so no one would see my most authentic self at 9:00 a.m. on the C train. All day at my office, I glanced over at the tote, a deviant grin spreading across my face at the thought of my secret friend lying in wait. That evening, I arrived at therapy and finally let Blackberry out.

"I brought someone," I said. My therapist looked genuinely excited.

I sat down on her sofa, and he perched on his hind legs, wagging his tail such that it thumped against the upholstery.

"Well he's adorable," she said. "Can I pet him?"

I nodded, and she reached toward us. But something must have scared Blackberry because when her hand went for the top of his head, he opened his mouth and bit her—hard, for a dog with human fingers as teeth anyway. At the time, I thought he was just being protective. He wasn't used to receiving acceptance from the outside (or the inside) world. Afterward, I felt guilty about this and later apologized. My therapist said it was okay—any self-respecting dog would have done the same.

For me, the question remains: How does a person who is constantly pushing people away "undo aloneness"? The urge for solitude is not in and of itself unhealthy, but I suppose what one does with it can be.

Like a dog chasing its tail, I often find myself chasing negative thoughts. Because they're there, I keep following them as if the exercise might result in something other than additional self-criticism. Perceiving one's self through a kaleidoscope of negativity is a downward spiral, a dizzying kind of misery to which my dog puppets provide an effective, albeit unusual, antidote. They're me but in disguise, which makes it much harder to criticize what they do or say and even how they look. For instance, when Waffles gets "back rolls" from his fabric bunching up, he covers his eyes with his little arms, embarrassed, but I secretly think they're cute.

Maybe loving a puppet can be a proxy for self-compassion.

Sometimes I treat Dog Mittens like wayward children. Other times, they bring out my own inner child. It makes me wonder if part of my desire for alternative motherhood is the urge to re-experience childhood, in all of its helplessness, from a place of power. When my husband and I are watching TV, Blackberry will get bored and suddenly cry out in a high-pitched voice, "I don't like this!" He then looks around as if expecting one of us to change the channel, which we inevitably do. It's not really rude because he's a puppet and doesn't appear to know any better. He is not constrained by the same veneer of social etiquette that I am.

Recently at a Pilates class, I was getting sick of doing stomach crunches when I heard Blackberry's voice in my head clearly say, "I don't like this!" I reflexively looked at my right arm to find my hand naked. I realized the sentiment would sound pretty ridiculous coming out of the mouth of an adult woman who had voluntarily signed up for the class. Still, the voice had a point. I actually hated working out and could pin most of the reasons I attended on decades of thinking some iteration of the same thought: *I should really look less lumpy.*

Maybe Blackberry carries my pent-up rage and therefore feels the need to bite on occasion. He is certainly a catalyst for honest emotion, which is one way of undoing aloneness. After all, there's nothing lonelier than carrying around bottled-up feelings. And though I'd like to think he's being playful when he bites my husband, it often carries same undercurrent of rage that drives the semi-maniacal act of tickling. He doesn't think; he just bites.

Sometimes my husband and I play with both puppets together. Since I started bringing them out of the bedroom with our pillows for TV time, he's taken a liking to Waffles.

"Everyone gets a dog," I'll say, swinging my black Lab by the foot and tossing the yellow one at him before plopping down on the couch to get comfortable. (Again, there are only two of us, but it feels good to point out when I'm being an egalitarian.) We watch television while Blackberry lies down on my lap wagging his tail and occasionally lifting his head up to look around before resting his chin on his front legs again.

Waffles is kind of a spaz, so he tends to spend a lot of time flying through the air, guided by my husband's arm, his front legs spread wide like an airplane. He likes to look at himself in the mirror that hangs on the wall next to our leather sofa, opening and closing his mouth awkwardly as if he is trying to extricate peanut butter from the roof of his mouth with his tongue. From my viewpoint at the other end of the couch, I get a fuller picture. It's an alternative portrait of togetherness that addresses my indefinable longing, although I'm not quite sure how. For now, I'm content to just let the puppets work their magic.

LOVERS

You find yourself moving forward in Google Street View on an avenue that cuts east to west across downtown Chicago. Your presence is silent and swift. The application requires you to move through traffic incrementally, an apparition in this faux reality of your choosing.

You're here because you just read an article in *Rolling Stone* about exposure therapy in which military veterans used virtual reality to safely experience and process PTSD triggers from combat zones. Under the supervision of a therapist, they talk through the feelings that come up—in order to create new neural pathways and ease future distress caused by their traumatic memories.

But you are not a soldier, and this is not Afghanistan. You are a thirty-five-year-old woman sitting in front of a computer monitor. Because you can see your city's skyline through a few leafless trees outside of your window, you feel safe enough to run your eyes along a two-dimensional map of the city you used to live in. On a whim, you enter Street View, and your pulse quickens. Your body doesn't seem to know that over a decade has passed.

Instinct tells you the apartment you're looking for is between Damen and Western, so you try that stretch of Hubbard Street first, losing yourself in the repetitive scenery as you go. Your eyes scan a three-flat red brick apartment building with a glass block window on the ground floor. Next to it sits a single-story warehouse with a garage door. This architectural arrangement, which you pass at least three times in ten blocks, makes you feel as if an invisible hand has reached out and grabbed you by the guts. What do you hope to gain by revisiting this place? You know no answers will be found via Google Maps. But you don't have anywhere else to look.

Your favorite outfit is a pair of slate blue wide-leg pants with subtle corduroy blocking at the knee and a pink shirt that wraps around the front and ties at the waist. It looks good with your tanned skin and blonde hair. You wear it with cork wedge sandals that have thin, lavender straps made of suede. You drink Campari and orange juice, shaken, out of a chilled martini glass. You smoke cigarettes and stay out until you can't remember you are the one who finished your pack.

It's late, but you are young. Twenty-three to be exact. You head out from a bar with a guy you know to smoke weed. He says his apartment is nearby, and you're not far from yours. Smoking will help you sleep soundly. You will forget that other guy who never texted you back, and your night will end at home alone, with you passed out in your clothes. Tomorrow you'll wake to find your roommate's runty pit bull waiting outside of your door, wagging her tail so hard it moves her entire back half. She loves you unconditionally, and it shows.

The guy driving your car has a tattoo on his neck of a rose and a skull. He's not exactly your type, but it's not him you're interested in, so you don't think too much about it. You pass the edges of the neighborhood you know and enter an empty part of Chicago that you don't. The open street-parking everywhere makes it feel soulless. "Tarot Readings," announces a sign on your left. The stoplights, red and green, bleed squiggles into the black sky every time your stick-shift car lunges forward through an intersection.

The tattoo guy parks your teal Honda at the curb, and you step out onto the street to find yourself in front of a brick building that looks like a garage. You follow him inside to a partially converted loft with concrete floors and exposed pipes. There is a single room in the front with a bed—and a second room in the back that looks like an unfinished basement, where two large Dobermans seem to have shit on the floor in several piles. You wonder exactly how long he's been gone.

This is so embarrassing, he says. *It's never happened before.*

Somehow you don't believe him. Now you are essentially just in his bedroom. He produces a bowl and some pot out of his dresser. You take a couple of hits. He works at a club across the street from the restaurant where you tend bar. When he comes in before his shift to buy a drink, he puts his money down, looks directly in your eyes and says *you can keep the change.* It is usually a very small amount that often includes actual change. While irksome, it doesn't register as any more annoying than how most men behave toward you. You ask him what he does outside of work.

I'm an artist, he says.

What kind?

Tattoo, he says. You lift up the side of your shirt three inches to show him a small tracing of ink on your ribs. It's a combination of yours and your best friends' initials, which together look like an infinity sign. He makes a sort of disgusted face at you—it's obvious he dislikes it. You don't really care since the feeling is mutual. His tattoos look as if they were plucked from a prepubescent boy's notebook—probably his. His knuckles have letters on them, but you're too afraid to find out what they say. You think it might be H-A-T-E.

You suddenly realize you are kind of fucked up and have no exit strategy. The tattoo guy decides he wants to make out with you, so you let him for a couple minutes. You really don't think you should drive but are not into taking this make-out session any further, so you decide to take a nap. You have bargained with your body enough for one night. Sleeping has always worked in the past to get dudes to leave you alone. Plus, you'll be able to drive in an hour or so.

I'm just going to chill for a sec before I go home, you tell him.

You lay your head down, and before you know it, you are sleeping soundly. Not only are you asleep, but you are having a sex dream. In the dream, you're with the guy you wanted to text you back earlier that night. He is supposed to just be your hookup but you recently realized you like him. In the dream, you are in his bed and can hear wind rustling the leaves outside of his window. You feel good, like you are lying on a beach in the Caribbean, and a warm tide is washing over the lower half of your body.

At some point, it occurs to you that you are not on a beach, you are on top of a strange bed in a strange apartment with concrete floors, your pants are unzipped, and there are tattooed hands in them. Your body and mind seem to be residing on two separate planets, and the signals between them are taking light years. Before you can reconcile the pleasurable feelings you're having with the person you don't want to be having them with, he is pulling off your pants off and replacing the flutter you felt from his hands with his tongue. Your body gives in and is rewarded with one giant wave that crashes over you, leaving you completely limp.

The tattooed hands use this opportunity to grab you by the hips and pull you toward the end of the bed. You look down just in time to see him undoing his pants and pushing himself inside of you. Your mind is now screaming. Within a few seconds, the rest of you catches up. *Stop, stop, stop,* you say. His eyes are vacant. You realize you are pleading with someone who doesn't even know that you're there. Your body is merely serving a function.

Finally, something appears to click inside of his brain.

He rolls off and lies next to you.

You wait for him to fall asleep before crawling out from under his arm. You tiptoe to the door and close it silently behind you. You readjust the driver's seat of your car and sit there, stunned. Your instinct is to light a cigarette, but you realize your hands are shaking. You put your keys in the ignition instead and start driving—past street names you know but somehow don't recognize. You feel like you are taking the darkest walk of shame in your life, except no one knows about it but you. Nor will they for a very long time.

When you get home, you try to enter your apartment as quietly as possible. You hear your roommate's pit bull stir at the clunking sound your wedge heels make against the wooden floors and wish she hadn't noticed your late entrance.

A month or so later, you are in bed with the guy who never texted you back that night and are so drunk you can't get off. You've been sleeping together for a while but only recently learned of his long-term relationship. *He has a girlfriend*, you think. *He doesn't love me*, you think.

Strangle me, you say. He presses his fingers into the tender skin above your clavicle and squeezes, but it is not enough. *Spit in my mouth*, you ask and then watch his saliva as it dangles down toward you. It's as if he's been cradling a tiny egg in his mouth, which he's now cracking open to share. It's the only special thing the two of you have together.

You tell yourself this is just the kind of shit you are into. You have no idea that your sudden urge to master your own degradation had to do with what happened in that brick building on the deserted street. The one you entered as one person and came out another. You can't begin to bear that loss yet, so you make up a new person to swallow both of your existing selves.

Eventually, he stops calling you altogether, and you settle on a new boyfriend who is ten years older than you and also a bartender. Your nickname for him is "Woobie," like a security blanket. When you decide you can no longer stand living in Chicago, he moves to New York to be with you. But once you're cohabiting in a shared apartment, you realize you never want to have sex with him again. This, you suppose, is partly because you're just not that attracted to him. But you also have begun questioning your sexuality.

You've noticed that you only like porn with women in it. If a penis shows up, it completely turns you off. So you binge watch the *The L Word*, secretly hoping you'll discover you're lesbian. But being gay never materializes—it's just a really good show.

When your doctor asks you what you use for birth control, you say, *avoiding sex.*

Well, you can't do that forever, she says.

Somewhere inside, you know this is true but aren't ready to accept it yet. So you decide to wait out your current relationship by refusing to have sex with your boyfriend until he finally hates you enough to not be mad when you break up with him.

Problem solved, you think—for now.

At twenty-seven, you fall in love with a man at your office. He sits at the desk next to you and tips his bag of snacking granola back like it's a cup, tapping the bottom when it's close to empty to make sure he gets every last cluster. You openly tease him about this, but that doesn't stop him from doing it.

Once when you're on your lunch break together, you're walking out of a Thai restaurant in Brooklyn when someone walks in with a dog that has the same dishwater blonde hair as he does.

Oh my god, that dog looks just like you, you say.

The dog proceeds to sniff his crotch, and his face turns red.

Aw, he likes you!

You can hear it in your own voice, but years later, he will tell you this is the moment he knew you liked him.

You begin spending weekends in his garden apartment drinking bottles of pinot noir in the kitchen and then retreating to his bedroom to take photos of yourselves kissing. You love being with him but find sex to be a little awkward. You can no longer flip the switch in your head you would normally flip to tell your body it's time to play the part of someone who's having sex. You feel more vulnerable with this person—this friend you are now falling in love with. You're afraid of what he would think if he saw you for who you really are.

So you end up drinking heavily. After six months or so, you notice you've begun to put on weight. One night, you are having wine and lying on your back in his bed, watching him kiss your stomach. You feel more than just your normal bodily insecurity. It is a creeping disgust. You feel like you're wearing your body as a suit and suddenly want to unzip it and leave it by the bedside. You feel smothered by something you can only identify as yourself. You decide to keep drinking until you black out and can't remember what happened next.

Years later, he tells you this is the first time you ever told him you were raped.

When you are thirty-three, you visit Chicago with the same man who is now your husband. He wants to know your old city—and doesn't quite understand why you hate it so much. You've told him fragments of what happened to you there, which you later minimized or recanted. Still, you shudder when you walk hand-in-hand past the restaurant you used to tend bar at. Later, by sheer chance, you drive down a deserted street, and your heartbeat quickens. It is the same feeling you get when you see a certain type of sleeve tattoos.

That night, you drink yourself into a stupor—and can barely make the taxi ride to the airport the next day without vomiting into the side pocket of the door. When you get home, you decide to tell your therapist, whom you've recently begun seeing for what you thought was unrelated anxiety. The rape has always been there in your mind, but like a corrupt file on a hard drive, your brain was unable to open it without professional help.

When you do finally access the memory in its entirety, it suddenly overwhelms your whole system. It is as if it just happened a few weeks before. You cry every day, like somebody just died. You can't focus on tasks as basic as writing an email. You don't even taste the roast chicken and vegetables your husband made you for dinner. This goes on for months. One night, you find yourself lying on your side facing the back of your leather couch, the rain beating down on your window air conditioner. You realize you can't imagine ever *not* feeling this way again.

Your therapist suggests that revisiting the memory might help you move on—if you're able to experience it differently. She says it's a commonly used technique, and you can even imagine a friend being there with you for support. You recoil from this idea because you are too ashamed. You fear you brought it on yourself, enjoyed it even. You don't want anyone else, however imaginary, to see you like that.

You think about it some more, and the only "friend" that comes to mind is your old roommate's little pit bull Olympia. She is small and brindle with a white belly and snout. When you lifted the comforter on your bed, she would burrow underneath it to cuddle with you as if on command. You were not sold on her at first because of your misconceptions about her breed. But she ended up proving you wrong.

You remember watching a show on television once where a large dog played nurse to a bunch of orphan kittens at a shelter. The dog wore a special vest and acted as a calming presence. When one fluffy orange kitten had bath time in a giant red bucket, the dog accompanied her into the room and lay on the ground nearby, remaining visible throughout the ordeal. During the bath, the kitten looked frozen in fear but kept her eyes on the dog. Afterward, she recovered immediately and began crawling happily on the dog again.

You hope your mental replay will go at least as well as dog-nurse-kitty-bath. But when you get up the nerve to finally try it with your therapist, you feel like you're living the memory all over again. It's not an out-of-body experience. You are not looking down on yourself from the ceiling. You are face-up on a bed.

Is Olympia with you? your therapist asks.

You see her wagging her tail, pacing back and forth on the floor next to you.

Yes, you answer. Olympia is now making a low gurgling noise, which normally precedes a high-pitched whine. It's her response to unexpected commotion, like your roommate play-wrestling with her boyfriend. She appears nervous but doesn't intervene, instead placing her paws in dog stretch pose, as if she might pounce but never does. You don't take your eyes off her, but in the periphery can see the dresser the pot came out of and a TV sitting on top of it. The room has taken on a sepia tint. You begin to feel nauseated.

I can't do this anymore. You open your eyes.

In bed with your husband, you're trying to enjoy yourself, or at least put on a convincing show so he can enjoy himself. But your mind is wandering, and you can't focus. Because you're not present, you can't experience pleasure. And because you're not experiencing pleasure, you suddenly have the feeling that your body is being used. It's like an empty shell you tried to abandon on the beach but couldn't because you were unable find a new one to occupy.

Your silence gives you away before the tears begin to fall.

This is the cycle. You cry during sex. Your husband stops. You try to recover from the episode and start again, but he is already getting dressed.

It happens so often you decide to go to a couple's sex therapist. The questionnaire at the intake appointment sends you into a panic. *Do you avoid, fear, or lack interest in sex? Do you approach sex as an obligation? Do you feel emotionally distant or not present during sex?* When you check nearly a dozen symptoms, you realize you have been living in complete denial. You are a loser, a failure, an idiot. You wonder why your husband hasn't left you already.

The therapist gives you homework—an exercise developed by Masters and Johnson, the duo made famous for their study of the sexual response. Every week, you and your husband lie in bed and touch each other sensually, which is not the same as sexually. You've never touched him, or anyone, like that—without an end goal in mind. So you feel like a weirdo at first, lightly rubbing your hand along his chest and down the side of his waist. He touches your back and thighs. Neither of you is supposed to talk, so you play the same instrumental Nels Cline album *Lovers* every time.

At first you leave your underwear on but find you get nervous anyway. Sometimes you get so anxious you cry and then have to stop, which surprises you. *Let's learn about this*, your sex therapist says almost every week. What you learn is that your brain is wired with a fight-or-flight response to any activity that could even be construed as sexual. Once it's triggered, you feel bad about yourself but try to hide it until you erupt in tears, after which point you feel even worse, because you think you have failed yet again.

Your sex therapist tells you *this* is the point of the exercise. To let the scared part of you come out and see that it's safe. *It's okay*, your husband learns to say—to reassure you so you don't feel bad. You eventually realize this is the self you have been holding underwater all this time, hoping she would drown. It should come as no surprise the process of coaxing her back out might take awhile.

While you're in sex therapy with your husband, you're also plugging ahead with your individual therapist, Judy, who you really like. She has dark, shoulder length hair with a few wisps of gray and a twinkle in her brown eyes. Judy is in her mid-fifties—not old enough to be your mother or young enough to be your contemporary, so you feel free of judgment when you're together.

You both take off your shoes in session and play with her office teddy bear. She is freewheeling and fun to talk to, not like other therapists you've had in the past, who sat in business suits, legs crossed, treating you like a specimen to be cut off at exactly ten minutes before the hour. She messages you videos of elephants in between sessions because she knows it is your favorite animal.

She's brought up the idea re-doing your memory again, of figuring out how to experience it in a way that would leave you feeling less ashamed. The mere mention of this makes you cry. You are tired of experiencing this memory over and over. Of that imagery invading your mind. It's been almost two years since you started talking about it—and twelve years since it happened.

But you trust her, so you close your eyes and you try. The second you are in that sepia-tinted bedroom with the dresser and the TV and the man on top of you and the pleasurable feelings you never wanted, you feel like screaming and ripping your entire body off. You can't do that, so you start crying hysterically, which is really only a default response because ripping your entire body off isn't physically possible.

She says, *Okay, I don't want to push you. We don't have to do it now.*

You hug her office bear, whose tag says his name is "Grizzles," and blow your nose, finishing her box of Kleenex. When you get home that evening, you just want to take a hot shower. You feel kind of like the kitty from dog-nurse-kitty bath, but your dog-nurse is a human man and he is currently watching TV in the living room with his feet up on the coffee table.

You are standing under your showerhead, allowing the hot water to beat against your shoulders when it happens: a flashback invades not only your mind but also your body. You see an image of a penis being forced inside of you, which is not particularly new as far as intrusive imagery goes. But this time, the memory is accompanied by a full bodily sensation. You can feel it happening and your knees buckle. Some time passes before your husband finds you crouched in a ball in the tub, the shower still running.

He gives you a towel, puts you in bed and lies next to you, trying to calm you down. But you are in hysterics. You try to stutter something out about the flashback, but your mind is already working on another message. It seems to be circling a fairly rudimentary truth that you've been too afraid to say aloud. Your lips form the words before you know what they are.

That man put his penis inside of me and now I'm afraid you won't want me anymore. You don't wait for his reaction. You jump out of bed, still soaking wet, and run back to the bathroom to put your head over the toilet to vomit. Nothing comes out. Instead you convulse, dry heaving for thirty seconds before collapsing onto the glossy tiles the two of you picked out together for the bathroom floor. They are cool against your skin, in a blue the color of the Mediterranean.

One day, shortly after your thirty-fifth birthday, you are meditating at a center near your office in Manhattan. It's helped you quiet your nervous thoughts. You're about twenty minutes into a relaxation session when two words pop into your head, as if out of nowhere: *ghost penis*. You assume it is a message from your subconscious about the significance of the flashback you experienced in the shower. It feels like a riddle you suddenly need to solve.

The next night, you go to see Judy at your individual therapy. You've been doing much better, and she brings up the idea of trying to revisit the memory again. She says you would be in complete control. She casually mentions you could do whatever you want, even if it's violent. You think this must be a sign. You are finally going to kill what has haunted you for so long. You will vanquish it from inside of you forever.

You lean in and lower your voice. *Could we Lorena Bobbitt him?*

She makes a serious face. *Yes.*

You tell her about your meditation session the night before. How the words just *flopped into your head*. You both giggle. *Freudian slip*, you say. You giggle some more.

She says you can bring anyone you want. Together you decide on an imaginary elephant, which you think would fit into the loft apartment. *Yeah, an elephant*, she says. *Their trunks are pretty strong.* You hadn't thought about that but agree it's true. Once, when you went to visit an elephant orphanage in Nairobi on vacation, you were standing in front of a two-year old calf in a stable when she extended her trunk out toward you. You thought it was adorable—until she grabbed your umbrella, pulled it through her gate and snapped it in a matter of seconds.

You wonder momentarily if it would be ethical to rope an imaginary elephant into a violent revenge fantasy. But you decide you'll cross that bridge when you come to it. You're more interested in the fact that elephants don't seem to feel shame. They walk around in skin that hangs off of their bodies like an oversized onesie. They roll in the mud naked without an inkling of insecurity. They live in groups that protect the young and vulnerable.

The next time you're in a session, you decide to give it a try. Immediately, you're in the apartment again, and your imaginary elephant—who is small for a full-grown female but still pretty big to be inside of a human dwelling— is distracting you from what's happening. She keeps one eye on you as she continues browsing for plants with her trunk, even though you're both standing on a concrete floor.

Out of the corner of your eye, you see a version of yourself on the bed with your knees bent and the dresser with the TV on top of it. You're in the middle of trying to unfreeze from the fear this scene is causing you when you remember that you are not required to stay.

I want to stop, you say, and then almost regret it.

You could have stayed longer this time but are beginning to wonder why this exercise isn't working for you. You think it might be because after so many years of denial, you have committed yourself to finding and understanding the truth. To try to revise the memory now, after you finally achieved such painful clarity, seems like it might somehow dishonor the journey it took for you to get here.

You decide if you do ever take an imaginary human with you to that scary apartment, it would be your husband. After six months of lying in bed touching each other in a non-sexual way and talking through all the feelings that come up, you realize he doesn't judge you. He doesn't think there's anything wrong with you. You're surprised to learn how attuned he is to your feelings— something you never would have known had your sex life not come crashing down around you.

One time, while doing your half-hour of weekly sensual touching, your mind wanders, and you start thinking about adopting a dog. That week at therapy, he says the exercise was "weird" and that you'd been "petting him like a dog." You laugh and tell him the truth—you were thinking about petting a dog. Another time, when you admit to the therapist you had a mini-flashback while he was touching you but didn't say anything because you didn't want him to know, he says he saw the goose bumps on your arm.

He picks up on almost everything, and you stop trying to protect him from any of it. You had no idea allowing someone else to see the parts of yourself that scare you the most—and love you even more for them—was exactly what you needed.

Your sex therapist can tell you've made progress and suggests you start touching each other in more overtly sexual places but still non-sexually. You don't really understand what this means, so he tries to help you imagine it. *What would it be like to just hold his penis in your hand?* You would normally laugh at this question, but suddenly you feel as if your mind is floating—like you're sitting on a leather couch having this therapy session under water.

You realize that you have never touched a penis without feeling pressure to "do something" with it. Normally, your approach would be to get in there, accomplish the mission, and get the hell out. You cannot even imagine what he is describing.

I would feel like a pervert, you say, *like I'm playing doctor*.

You agree to try it anyway. But as soon as the penis holding is introduced into your weekly routine, you somehow manage to avoid doing your sex therapy homework for three weeks. And it's not just you. Your husband complains of headaches or being tired when Sunday night rolls around, the weekly time slot you've set aside for this. You suspect it would be much easier on both of you to stay in this safe and happy dog-petting zone for the time being.

While you're struggling to move forward in sex therapy, you also feel stuck in your own therapy. You've been trying for over two years to re-do that painful memory without any success. You tell Judy about the article you read in *Rolling Stone* about exposure therapy. How you went to Google Street maps to find the red brick apartment. How it made your blood run cold.

She says the point of revisiting the memory is not to trigger yourself over and over but to bring the resources you have now back to help your younger self, who had to keep this secret all alone. In order to do this, you first have to be able to uncouple current you from past you—the one who experienced the trauma. You understand this in theory but in practice find it hard to accomplish. She suggests instead of visiting that apartment again, you invite your younger self to visit you here, in her Manhattan office.

You have no idea how to do it, but you close your eyes and try.

Imagine she's sitting in that chair, Judy says.

You feel silly doing this at first, but slowly you begin to see her.

What does she look like? Judy asks.

She has long blonde hair and is wearing her favorite outfit: a pair of slate blue pants and a pink shirt that wraps and ties in the front.

What is she doing?

She is smoking a cigarette and laughing. She is clearly in a good mood. This makes you cry, and at first you don't know why. Later, you realize it's because you feel bad for her, about the loss she will soon endure, and the years of confusion and sadness that will follow.

It finally occurs to you that the work you are doing to heal yourself psychologically has less to do with purging some phantom from your past and more to do with caring for the version of yourself who never got the love and attention she deserved.

A few weeks later, you're talking about penises again in sex therapy, but this time it doesn't make you squeamish. You haven't had a flashback in a while and feel up to taking the next step, whatever it may be.

What is the first thing that comes to mind when you think of a penis? your sex therapist asks. *That thing I have to touch,* you say, without stopping to think you might be offending your husband. Honestly, it has nothing to do with him; you've never been a big fan. Or is that just what you've been telling yourself? You're not sure anymore.

In the past, you wouldn't have been nervous about touching your husband, but now that you've started your sex life over, it seems like an important step you don't want to screw up. The following Sunday, when you're rubbing your hand along his waistline, and you almost do it but lose your nerve. He teases you afterward. He says he could tell you were considering it but decided against. You feel like a teenager, and your face flushes in embarrassment.

The next week, when he sets up a jazz record and climbs into bed, you already have a plan. After about ten minutes, you make a move and hold his penis in your hand for about thirty seconds, even though this is excruciatingly awkward. You think to yourself that it feels friendly. He looks incredibly uncomfortable, a small grimace forming across his face, and you don't blame him. You assume it's due to the awkwardness, but he later explains he was trying to avoid getting an erection. He didn't want to scare you away. You decide those must have been the friendly vibes you picked up on.

The next week, while lying on a couch Judy's office, you decide to pay a visit to your twenty-three-year-old self back in Chicago. She was fired from the restaurant that the tattooed man used to come into and now works at a different bar in another neighborhood. She never understood precisely why she was let go, but it occurs to you she was probably going through a pretty difficult time—with no one to talk to.

You tell Judy she has to sit in the imaginary car. You think your younger self might be spooked by your glasses and your sensible shoes as it is. So you mentally enter the bar alone to find her at a table in the back, smoking a cigarette on her break. She's changed her hair, you notice. It's darker, and she now has bangs.

If you could give her something, what would it be? Judy asks from the floor beside you.

You don't have to think about this at all. You reach into your imaginary bag and pull out a brown stuffed dog, like one the two of you had when you were little. You bet she would like to sleep with it.

What is her reaction?

She likes it, you say. You picture her smiling with her arms folded across the dog, hugging it. She's making the same face she did in a photo from her twenty-first birthday, except then she was wearing a party hat.

Do you think it will make her feel better?

You don't have to think about this either.

I know it will.

You open your eyes.

If you were to ask my husband about my sleep habits, he would tell you how I kick and punch, how I speak in tongues—how I even try to shove him out of our double bed. "You slept like a total maniac last night," he'll say nearly every weekend, coffee mug in hand, as he tries to hide his smile. I usually protest, though I know it happens far too often to be hyperbole.

I've always been afraid of the dark, including the one brought on by the back of my eyelids. Even as a child, I recognized it as the harbinger of nightmares. But like my own unconscious mind, it was never really the darkness I feared so much as what I imagined might be hiding in it. My parents, tired of me running into their bedroom in the middle of the night complaining of monsters in my closet or imaginary spiders crawling across my feet, relocated me semi-permanently into a second twin bed in my older sister's room.

She slept like a log while I stared at the ceiling.

Every night, my father would come upstairs to put us to bed, but we didn't go quietly. Instead, we played twenty questions—or as many as we could squeeze in before he noticed we were flattering his intelligence and enforced our bedtime. Sometimes we'd ask questions we thought were silly just to waste time, like, "If a tree falls in the woods, does it still make a sound?" Other times, we'd ask harder ones, along the lines of, "How do I know what you see as the color green is the same thing I see as the color green?"

The line of inquiry that unsettled me most was always existential in nature. I wanted to know, even at a young age, what we were all doing here anyway.

"What is outer space made of?" I asked.

"Nothing," my father said.

"You mean, like air?"

"No," he explained. "Air is made of molecules."

My father, being a science geek, took the time to break down the carbon dioxide and oxygen content of the earth's atmosphere vs. the nonexistent content of empty space. I stared out the window at the black sky between the stars, my hands searching underneath the sheets as I tried to grasp this newfound concept. My tiny twin bed hosted an army of stuffed animal friends, but when I looked at them for comfort, they just stared back at me blankly.

By that time, I had come to understand that my place in the universe was not unlike the Whos of Whoville who lived on a tiny speck of dust in the clover field of the Dr. Seuss story. My scientific discovery—what I began to think of simply as "nothingness"—made the idea that a benevolent character like Horton would be listening for our voices and looking out for our well-being seem even less likely than it had before.

Once I got to high school, I learned in physics class that sound requires the presence of molecules to travel, and therefore pockets of deep space would remain silent as long as they remained empty. But what of the absence of sound, then—did it make a noise? I supposed not, unless someone were there to actually listen for it.

As a teenager, I fell for my boyfriend Jack who, although dense, "understood" me in the sense that he provided the weed I needed to stop thinking about eternal nothingness. At some point, he must have learned to fill the void in his brain with alcohol and fighting. He was like a black hole—a vacuum that destroyed whatever got close enough to be sucked in. He hadn't hidden the fact that he'd been violent with other men, nor had he flaunted it.

In the beginning, he was nice to me. And then suddenly, he wasn't.

My ex-boyfriend, this chunk of the universe that ended up at my front door, eventually became the object of my adult nightmares. In them, he boasted some major advantage other than just his sheer size. He'd be driving a truck, and I'd be traveling by roller-skates. He'd be chasing me through the woods with a gun, and I'd be hiding in them naked. He'd have regular ground to traverse, and I'd be stuck in quicksand—my chances of escape sinking with every step.

Eventually, after putting enough time and space between us, the nightmares eased but never stopped altogether. Perhaps this is because this concept of space-time forms a giant inescapable net. In order to rid myself of him entirely, I'd have to travel back in time. According to the theory of relativity, in order to move backward on the space-time continuum, one must be moving faster than the speed of light. That is to say, one must move forward into the dark—in order to move backward into the light.

I essentially did this in trauma therapy.

After a couple years of exploring dark, uncharted corners of my mind, the nightmares morphed slowly into dreams. In one of the later versions, I found myself exploring the rooms of an unfamiliar house only to turn and find my ex-boyfriend on a leash beside me—well, the essence of him anyway. His upper torso had been replaced by the front half of a porpoise. As a half-man, half-dolphin, he was less threatening in that he couldn't talk with his beak or punch anyone with his fins. He didn't make any of those weird clicking noises. Instead, he followed me around like silent baggage—a fear I could never quite untether myself from.

Discovering him next to me was like swimming somewhere off the coast of Florida and catching the silhouette of a manatee out of the corner of your eye. In an instant, your heart would stop, your life would flash before your eyes, and you would accept your bones were about to be pulverized by a monster's teeth. Only after recognizing some humanity in the face of the swimming mammal would your heart rate slow. The words "sea cow" would settle into your head like sediment into a riverbed, and eventually, silt into the sea.

According to *Scientific American*, the same mirror neurons responsible for coding and imitating violent behavior also engender empathy—through recognition of facial expressions and other nonverbal gestures. Oddly, the mechanism that makes us biologically suitable for civilization also threatens our individual survival. How is it that violent and empathic impulses are so entwined? And why do we go to such lengths to shield ourselves from the truth about what it means to be human?

Growing up, my family went to church every week. Sunday mornings, I'd be forced into a black velvet dress and itchy white tights so that the four of us could get into our blue Chevy Suburban and make the eight-minute drive to Second Presbyterian Church. I'd go straight to a room upstairs to attend something called "Sunday School" where children received short lessons about Christ and then made crafts that said things like, "Jesus loves us" using glue sticks, glitter, and paper plates.

I thought I might get more information on the Jesus stuff by going to the adult sermons, but I never did. Instead, I'd sit between my parents and alternate between staring blankly at my patent leather Mary Janes and flipping through the hymnal in search of an interesting song to read. When I was in elementary school, my father stopped going to church altogether. When I asked my mother why I still had to, she said, "He's an adult and you're a child."

In fifth grade, when I went through Confirmation, the official rite of passage to becoming a member of the church, I took the opportunity to question whether my religious beliefs were indeed mine. The idea of committing to a god who may or may not exist and having faith he'll take care of you in the afterlife seemed like putting a lot of eggs in one basket, even to a ten-year-old. I didn't understand why I needed some fuddy-duddy scripture, a man with gray hair in a robe, and a lot of burgundy carpet just to tell me not to be a jerk.

In the end, it was the church's refusal to acknowledge science—a marker for the progress of humanity—that tipped me over the edge.

By middle school, I started staying home with my father every Sunday. Eventually, I asked him about the one piece that's missing from the atheist package.

"What happens when we die?"

"Nothing," he said. "You're dead."

Theoretically, it made sense, but I couldn't imagine it in practice, so instead I imagined the closest thing I could think of—that moment when you're about to fall asleep and you see another realm of darkness approaching beyond the inside of your eyelids. What scared me most about his answer was that I agreed it was probably true. Christian theology offers an out: if you live by the teachings of Jesus and have faith in God, your soul will be resurrected after death. But it seemed too easy.

Buddhism, on the other hand, says that there is no soul—only a stream of consciousness that carries from one life to the next. It's an unsatisfying cycle in which liberation can only be achieved through enlightenment. When I studied the philosophy in college, I found it comforting somehow. If you could truly come to accept that "life is suffering," the idea of nothing might start to seem almost like a relief.

If death were the endless darkness of outer space—a place only a handful of people have seen for what doesn't even amount to a mere blip in the lifetime of the universe, then sleep would be like the ocean—a miniature version of an alien world that we explore in small dives, imaginary bouts of wakefulness we call dreams.

Not long ago, I dreamed I was swimming in the ocean and everything was pitch black. But I wasn't lost, nor was I afraid. I thought I had achieved some higher plane of consciousness—or even a kind of clairvoyance. When I awoke, I realized I had dreamed of being an orca, which meant I was using sonar to "see" without sight.

Being an apex predator would have its upsides. For one, you wouldn't have to live in fear, at least not of anything other than humans. Because the Buddhist mind stream is said to move among the spirit, animal, and human realms, I even wondered if I'd been an orca in a past life. I'd also recently watched *The Whale*, a documentary about an orca named Luna who became separated from his family as a baby and trapped in the Nootka Sound off of Vancouver Island. Animal rights activists had attempted to free him but were in conflict with a native tribe who believed that his presence signified the return of a chief who had recently died.

Orcas are social animals, so Luna tried making friends with humans. He would approach boats and pop his glossy black head out of the water to say hello. He seemed almost otherworldly—this alien just trying to make contact with life on land. In the process, he did a fair amount of damage around the local marinas by ripping the rudders off of boats. He also liked to swim alongside them and rub his body against their hulls, a substitute for the contact he would have had with his pod had he not been orphaned.

Eventually, he was sucked in by a boat propeller and died from his injuries.

One man interviewed in the documentary who had made eye contact with Luna after he popped his head up out of the water said he could tell there was "somebody home" in there. I knew what he meant; I could see it through the screen. Inside of Luna was something that went beyond molecules and buoyancy and the acceleration that he'd need in order to hit an ice sheet from below and knock his next meal into the water.

In trauma therapy, when I didn't have the right words, my therapist would ask me to describe how my emotions felt physically. Recognizing Luna's—I'll call it "personhood"—landed like a warm pang in the right side of my chest, just above my diaphragm. This ray of hope I felt reaching into me must have been the opposite of the pool of shame one feels after committing an act of violence. It seemed like an SOS from another spaceship, signaling that I'm not alone in this vast, empty universe after all.

Before a tornado hits, the pressure drops and the sky turns green. If you're in its path, you'll hear it roaring like a freight train. In Illinois, when the sirens went off at night, my whole family would go downstairs to huddle together in the crawl space with an AM radio and a flashlight, doing our best to avoid the many daddy long-legs who'd taken up residence there. It was a ritual we practiced more religiously than actual religion.

But hurricanes were unfamiliar territory.

When Superstorm Sandy pummeled the Eastern Seaboard, I lived with my husband in a ground floor apartment near the water. He slept peacefully while I lay in bed, my eyes wide open, listening to the wind—waiting for something to happen. Overnight, the water crept up, flooding homes, restaurants, and even the subway stations. Our apartment was high enough up be spared, but by the next morning, broken planks, tree branches, and even dead rats had washed up onto our block.

It was a reminder that eventually we'll all be returned, piece by piece, to the swirling matter of the universe from which we sprung.

The day after the storm, I watched a golden retriever digging through the debris. He lifted his shiny head to reveal a prize—in the form of a dead rat. The woman at the other end of the leash began shrieking.

In the weeks that followed, I couldn't get this image out of my head. I would be lying in bed and suddenly wonder what it would feel like to have a wet dead rat in my mouth. As soon as the thought came into my mind, I'd squint, stick my tongue out, and make the kind of "pleh" noise you do when you're standing over the sink trying to get the taste of sour milk out of your mouth.

It bothered me so much that I went to a psychiatrist, who gave me medication that helped, but it also gave me double vision and "brain zaps," which feel just like they sound. It's difficult to know if the rat obsession, which eventually passed, was indeed pathology or just part of the collateral damage of owning a brain. Within the mental tornado of ideas and images, some are bound to be disturbing enough to stick, given the kind of world that created them.

The first time I ever meditated was in a chair in front of my bedroom window overlooking the East River. I sat down, closed my eyes, and found myself floating in what seemed like empty space. The only thing grounding my mind to my physical body was the rhythm of my breath—inhales and exhales advancing and receding like the tide.

It was terrifying.

In the beginning, I could barely hold off my thought storm for thirty seconds. After a few months, I gained the ability to handle five minutes, then ten, then fifteen. The point of my meditation practice was to acknowledge the content of my thoughts without identifying with it. Instead, I would imagine every notion, however strange or mundane, as if it were just floating by on an asteroid. As a therapeutic tool, this proved valuable. But it also seemed to be leading me back to where I started.

If our thoughts are not representative of who we are—then who are we?

"Collections of atoms," I can imagine my father saying, without even looking up from his breakfast. There is something comforting about certainty, even when the object of it is so unsatisfying. Still, I have a lot of questions.

ACKNOWLEDGEMENTS

I would like to thank all the publishers, editors, teachers, family members, and friends who encouraged me and supported my work. I am immensely grateful. Many of the essays were first published in literary magazines.

"On the Edge of Seventeen" *Guernica*

"The Diving Well" *Creative Nonfiction*

"Before Empowerment" *Longreads*

"Apollo's Revelation" *Nat Brut*

"Virtues of Plop" *The Cut*

"The Endless Container" *Fanzine*

"A Woman, a Plan, an Outline of a Man" *Jezebel*

"Everyone Gets a Dog" *The Smart Set*

"Lovers" under the title "Nurse Dog" *The Normal School*

"Orcas in Space" *Vol. 1 Brooklyn*